WRITING UP YOUR FAMILY HISTORY

a do-it-yourself guide

D0106611

WRITING UP
YOUR FAMILY
HISTORY

a do-it-yourself guide

John Titford

COUNTRYSIDE BOOKS
NEWBURY BERKSHIRE

First published 1996 in conjunction with the Federation of
Family History Societies as *Writing and Publishing Your Family History*
Second edition 2003
© John Titford 1996, 2003

COUNTRYSIDE BOOKS
3 Catherine Road
Newbury, Berkshire

To view our complete range of books,
please visit us at
www.countrysidebooks.co.uk

ISBN 1 85306 822 5

Cover design by Peter Davies,
Nautilus Design

Produced through MRM Associates Ltd., Reading
Printed by Woolnough Bookbinding Ltd., Irthlingborough

CONTENTS

Do you have a shoe box full of old photographs? (Above, left) Arthur and Annie Buckler, the author's maternal grandparents, on the day of their wedding, 1897; (above) Benjamin Titford, silversmith and pawnbroker, poses for a photograph in the studio of Lock and Whitfield, Regent Street; he was born in 1814, before the Battle of Waterloo; (left) Harry, Sidney and Doris Titford, the three children of Henry James and Margaret Titford of North London, photographed in about 1912.

WHY WRITE A
FAMILY HISTORY?

Why would anyone in his or her right mind want to write a family history, let alone publish it? I ought to be dissuading you from doing any such thing. It will cost you a great deal of effort, and could prove very tiring; it could be an expensive undertaking if you want it to be; it could put strains on your relationship with your nearest and dearest; you might not even be happy with the final product once you've brought it to completion. Have I dissuaded you? In a world which often seems to be aware of the price of everything and the value of nothing, you might think that only people who really are out of their minds would embark on such an enterprise.

And yet people do it – regularly, and in increasingly large numbers. Why? Here comes the good news. Writing your family history could be one of the most rewarding things you ever do – with rewards measured in terms of personal satisfaction, not financial gain. You may soon discover that there's a book or a series of short articles inside you just bursting to get out; with luck you'll tap the deepest springs of your creativity and give the lie to those teachers at school who gave you low marks for English composition. You'll give pleasure to members of your immediate family, and your name and the work you've done could well be featured on the Internet, with the result – if you're lucky – that distant cousins you never knew you had will contact you from all over the globe in gratitude and astonishment at your achievement, be it ever so modest. Perhaps most important of all, you'll feel that you've paid an appropriate and lasting tribute to your ancestors, those individuals who have long since departed this mortal life but have helped to make you what you are. How could you *not* write a family history?

SEIZE THE DAY

Carpe diem – that is, seize the day, grab the opportunity while you can – could well stand as our text for this book. Without being too morbid about it, we could say that what you intend to do in life, you should start doing today – since none of us has an infinite number of tomorrows.

I can still vividly recall a conversation which took place a few years ago on a plane which was carrying a group of English family historians to Salt Lake City, where we were to take part in a study tour organised by *Family Tree Magazine*. Two friends of mine from the group were deep in conversation with a couple of charming ladies from the Church of Jesus Christ of Latter-day Saints. The ladies were intrigued, and quizzed my friends as to their intentions: 'Why are you visiting Salt Lake City?'; 'To collect information about our ancestors'; 'Oh! And what will you do with it all once you get it? We're Mormons, and family history information is of great importance to us, so we know exactly what *we* do with it – but what about you?'

This, then, is my question, too. You've collected lots of information about your family. Now what will you *do* with it all?

AN EXHORTATION

My exhortation to you is this: do think seriously about writing your own family history, and do think about writing it right now. You could make a lot of people – including yourself – very happy and fulfilled in the process. As family historians we are in the posterity business – we thrive on what others have left behind. We probably read enough wills to know that you don't really own anything in this life; whatever you have is yours in trust for the duration of this life, and then passes to someone else after you've gone. What will you leave behind for posterity? Will it be a family history that might be read and enjoyed by others for many years to come? I do hope so.

There are several ways of publishing information about your family which others can read and enjoy. You may like the idea of a regular family journal or news-sheet, and you could even issue a substantial family history in parts over a period of time. Here I'm going to assume that you'd like to aim at something even more substantial – a full-length family history, published as a book. If your preferred option is to publish on the Internet, I'll have a few words to say about that, too.

One of the most enthralling aspects of writing a family history is the way in which it's possible to breathe new life back into your ancestors. So a real event which happened in the past – a marriage, for example – might be recorded on a sheet of paper or parchment; from that written record it's possible to re-create the original event in your imagination. Put your imaginative picture into words in a family history, and you've given your ancestors that most precious of gifts, the one that men and women have sought for thousands of years – a touch of immortality. It's worth the effort, believe me!

There are probably as many different approaches to family history as there are family historians. Some love to collect information and tuck it away like squirrels hoarding nuts; others are only happy when the genealogical programme on the computer is in full swing; others like to spend time quietly contemplating the past and the people who have inhabited it. If you pay a visit to the library of the Society of Genealogists, in London, indulge in a spot of people-watching. Most varieties of family historian are there – from the frenetic gleaner of information, high on nervous tension and rushing around as much as it's possible to rush in such an environment, to the slow reader who seems to be in danger of falling asleep at any moment.

Collecting information – data, if you prefer – about your family is what I think of as high-octane work. As you scan the pages of a parish register or skim through the wording of a will, the engines are firing on all cylinders. It can be exciting and stimulating – which is why so many family historians come back for more, addicted to the adrenal flow of it all.

By contrast, it looks as if the act of disciplining yourself to write down your findings in an ordered way, as a family narrative, might be far less rewarding – boring, even. Not a bit of it! I'll run the risk of being thought rather prescriptive here, and say that if you have only collected data about your family (ancestor spotting, we may call it) and stored the information away safely somewhere, you've only done half a job – or less.

Advertisements in family history journals which make proud announcements such as 'Bloggs family: 65,000 references on a database' both impress and depress me all at the same time. Surely there is more to family history than this? You have 65,000 references? Wonderful! Now what will you *do* with all that information?

The ideal and complete process, in my view, is this: to collect data; to analyse it (that is, to make sense of it all) and finally to synthesise it (that is, to put it all together so that it has some overall meaning). If you've followed this process through to the end, then writing a family history would be a natural outcome and should not prove too difficult a task. The fact is that writing your family history is also high-octane work; not only that, but the process of pulling all the threads together into a coherent narrative will lead you on to greater discoveries. There will be new questions to be answered, new avenues to explore; your research programme could benefit enormously.

WHY *NOT* TO WRITE A FAMILY HISTORY: YOUR EXCUSES

The trick about writing a family history, of course, is that you have to get started. Why not straight away? Here the excuses will come thick and fast, so let's examine a few:

◆ *I have no time*

Is time something you have, or something you make? If you say you have no time to do a particular job, what you're really saying is that other tasks must take priority. Of course they must. It would be foolish in the extreme to abandon all your responsibilities to your immediate family just to closet yourself away for weeks and emerge with a completed family history. What you *can* do, however, is to salvage a moment here, an hour there, even a day or a week in order to get your project underway. Perhaps you could get up earlier in the morning for a few days and put in an hour or two's work before the rest of the world is up and about? If early morning is a bleary-eyed time for you, try grabbing a short spell or two at some other point in the day.

In any case, you probably already spend a fair bit of time on family history matters? New avenues of investigation open up all the time and are practically infinite as one thing leads to another; why not curtail your research programme for a while, and get your adrenal fix from doing a bit of writing?

◆ *My research isn't finished yet*

I can't write a family history yet, you may say, because I haven't done a million and one tasks like checking the bishop's transcripts for Hephzibah Gotobed's burial.

Goodness me, I hope your family history research will never be finished! What could be worse? Take heart. No piece of historical writing can ever be complete and definitive for all time, and he'd be a fool that would tell you otherwise. All history is conjecture: what we need is information, not completion; truth, not total neatness. And not even the 'whole truth', either, but just that part of it which you have the time and energy to deal with. Do aim to be like a lawyer: work to a specific and defined brief.

James Joyce's original title for the novel which eventually became *Finnegans Wake* was simply *Work in Progress* – and that is what your account of your family will be. The best you can do is to present a snapshot in time, an account of what you know so far. You will no doubt discover a vital piece of information concerning your family the day after your book is published, and will probably be tempted to say, 'If only I'd waited'. Eschew all such temptation. Your research won't come to an end, I hope, just because your book has been written. Maybe you'll even produce a revised edition or a second volume one day?

All this is nothing new. As long ago as the seventeenth century, Richard Baxter, the well-known Presbyterian divine, was writing:

No man doth anything so well, but it might be better done

11

and in the 1750s Dr Johnson has this to say in the preface to his famous dictionary:

> *Thus to pursue perfection was, like the first inhabitants of Arcadia, to chace* [sic] *the sun, which, when they had reached the hill where he seemed to rest, was still beheld at the same distance from them.*

It will always feel like the wrong time to put your ideas into print. Tomorrow your family history will be complete, or so you believe – but tomorrow, so the cliché runs, never comes. If you're the kind of person who only feels comfortable with total neatness, then you'll have a problem. The fact is that family history is all about the lives and relationships of real people – and real people, in the last analysis, are not subject to being packaged and 'databased' in a way that might suit our yearning for tidiness. We'll have to learn to live with uncertainties, loose ends, unanswered questions – all very frustrating, but the rules of the game, I'm afraid.

The paradox which underlies all this is as follows: to write a good family history, you have to be a perfectionist but also a realist. Set yourself high standards of accuracy, but be honest about what you can and cannot achieve.

◆ *I'm no good at writing*

You don't need to be a Shakespeare or a Milton to write a family history. It may be a long time since you wrote anything of any substance, and they may have done little to boost your confidence when you were at school, but you're almost certain to surprise yourself once you get going. A dictionary could be a great help, but if you want to expand your vocabulary or to find a word that has temporarily escaped you, you can't beat a thesaurus (cheap enough to buy, these days), which groups words of similar meaning together and could be your constant desk-side companion.

Don't be hoodwinked into thinking that some people can just sit down and write flowing English with no effort. A fluent writer, like a concert pianist, may start with a natural talent but will have to supplement it with a great deal of hard graft – a truth realised in the 18th century by Alexander Pope:

True ease in writing comes from art, not chance.
(*Essay on Criticism*, 1711)

Here's another paradox, then: if you want your writing to look effortless, you'll have to put a great deal of effort into making it look that way. You can generally reckon that a good piece of writing consists of 10% inspiration supplemented by 90% perspiration.

By all means enrol for a course at your local college if you really feel you could do with a boost, or follow a distance learning programme, working from home.

Above all, don't be intimidated – have a go!

◆ *My typewriter's broken*

A pretty feeble excuse, eh? Well get it mended. Or, if you like, write your story in longhand and then pay someone to type it up for you. Better still, see if you can afford a decent computer with a word processing package. A word processor will allow you to add text, remove it, reposition it, correct it or modify it at will. You really owe it to yourself to go for this option if you possibly can. The typewriting alternative can be messy by comparison, I'm afraid – you'll probably need to use correcting fluid, correcting paper, scissors, paper and glue. Not to be recommended!

Do aim for a PC or an Apple Mac computer if you possibly can. There is a great variety of word processing software available on the market. I've always found that Word Perfect suits my needs very well, though many of my friends swear by Microsoft Word and other programmes. Shop around.

As the word-processor text for your family history increases in size, you may have to decide whether to keep it all together, or whether to split it into smaller documents, each consisting of sections, chapters or parts, which will be easier to work with.

You won't forget to save your computer text on a regular basis, will you? A power cut or a thunderstorm could wipe away a few hours' work if you're not careful, and you'd be well advised to save each day's work onto a 'floppy' in case the hard disk decides to die over night.

NAME	Age.	Ward.	ADMITTED.	DISCHARGED.	REMARKS.
Tierney, Jane	7	12	July 18. 1826	July 22 1826	To Enfield
Tierney, John	4	12	" "	" "	do
Tierney, James	2	13	" "	" "	do
Tarling, Eliz th	70	19	" 27	Nov r 22	Absconded
Taylor, Jaffry	50	8	" 28	Dec r 5	Himself
Trelman, Ephriam	20	8	Aug t 17		
Tarr, Sarah Ann	19	22	" 18	Aug t 22 1826	Absconded
Titford, Eliz th	48	16	" 22	25 "	
Thompson, Fred k	15	8	" 26	Aug t 28. 1826	To the H s of Corr for refusing to work
Tennant, John	21	6	Sept r 4	Nov r 11	Absconded
Temple, Maria	12	12	" 7	Oct r 11 1826	By O of H. to Norton Falgate
Thompson, Fred k	15	8	" 11	Oct r 12 1826	To M r Hillier Lambeth S t Bow
Turrell, Susannah	41	16	" 22	April 11 1827	
Thompson, W m	52	3	" 29	May 29 1829	Died
Trindle, Harriet	43	23	Oct r 17	Feb y 15. 1827	To S t Bartholomews Hospital
Trindle, Gregory	21	8	" "	April 20 1827	with 2/ To do
Tennant, James	45	8	" "	April 14 1827	with 5/ Work
Tennant, Rebecca	43	26	" "	" " "	"
Tennant, Lucy	17	12	" "	Dec r 21 1826	To Service
Tennant, Charles	10	1	" "	July 22. 1827	

It is the 'ordinary' families that are increasingly used to illustrate our national history. (Admissions register, Shoreditch Workhouse, London, 1826. London Metropolitan Archives P91/LEN/1336.)

If you look ahead to the day when your family history will finally be complete, you may well decide at that stage to hand over a disk to a commercial printer, and get him to print it in book form for you. Much software these days is inter-compatible, but a quick telephone call or visit to the printer to discuss the viability of the word processing programme you will be using might be a good idea. A local photocopying agency or bureau may also be happy to accept your work on disk, on a CD, or even via the Internet.

In the event, you might not wish to go to the expense of buying some new software just to be able to produce your book more readily at the end, but do give this matter some thought before you start merrily typing away.

◆ *My family story is so very ordinary*

Good! That's what we need! Most famous people and famous families – and not a few infamous ones, too – have already had their biographers. The world doesn't really need too many more books about the Churchills and the Brontës, but you will quite probably be writing the first ever published account of your more modest family. That would be a real achievement. Historians and demographers are increasingly interested in stories of 'ordinary' families, which make up the great bulk of the population. In any case, most family histories include a significant smattering of individuals who have been far from ordinary, no matter what their station in life may have been.

◆ *I don't know which ancestral line to write about*

Initially, focus upon one and only one line. Make a choice – but start somewhere ...

Any more excuses? No? Good – let's get started.

PREPARING TO WRITE YOUR FAMILY HISTORY

COLLECTING MATERIAL: THE FOREGROUND

What kind of material will you collect as a basis for your family history?

If it is to have maximum impact, your completed family history should contain two elements which are inter-related. In the foreground will be the individuals whose lives will form the main focus of the story, but these lives will be played out against the broader background of the historical period through which the people lived. A good family history, in other words, should quite literally be an account of the *lives* and *times* of your ancestors.

Let's think about the foreground first.

◆ *A family archive*

I do hope you'll have at least the rudiments of your own private family archive? A family bible, perhaps, or a photograph album, baptismal certificates, an unsorted pile of granny's papers, letters or diaries (some too intimate and private ever to use in your story?), a bundle of old photographs or a pair of cuff links with engraved inscriptions. Or perhaps, if you're unlucky, almost nothing at all?

Perhaps you'll have notes taken from in-depth interviews with elderly relatives, or tape-recordings of the same? You may have jotted down some family legends and traditions which will need evaluating and sifting for any grain of truth each might contain: 'One ancestor was a pirate', 'We came over with the Huguenots', and so on.

◆ *Your own life story*

Will your own biography form part of your story? We will all become part of history one day – if we're not already! – and there is a strong argument for telling your own tale if you feel brave enough. You're hardly going to bare your soul and confess all your misdeeds, are you, but this could be a good chance to share your disappointments as well as your achievements with others. Editing here will be crucial; presumably each of us could ramble on about our own lives for several pages.

Do try to think of all the little details that will give flavour to your own personal story. What small, almost insignificant, things were different when you were a child? Did people leave their front door open or unlocked? Was the milk delivered on a horse-drawn dray? Was sugar sold in blue paper bags and toothpaste in flat tins? Did your bag of crisps contain a small twist of blue paper containing salt? Did you need rationing coupons to buy sweets? Was butter patted before you bought it? Did mother make junket? Did father buy Capstan Full Strength cigarettes without tips, or a packet of five Woodbines, or did he have a tin full of shag for his pipe? Did he give you the 'fag cards' to flick at school? Did your local drapery store have a system of overhead wires used for conveying an order and cash in little round pots to a central cashier? Did you have a Co-op number for your 'divi'? And if so, can you still remember what it was? (Bet you can!) Were there ceramic inkwells sunk into your school desk? Did you have a snake-shaped fastener on your trouser belt? Did your grandmother call linoleum 'oil cloth'? (Mine did!)

Jot down memories like this – you might be surprised how many you come up with. Feature such apparently insignificant details in your autobiography – they will add flavour to what you have to say. After all, your abiding memory of the year 1956, for example, may not be that there was a Suez Crisis going on at

Deaths.

H. Parkes died 6th March 1854

H. J. Titford died 3rd March 1862

E. Parkes died 12th January 1882

B. Titford died 10th October 1879

Hannah Hollings 23rd April 1894

Sarah Medlicott 6th January 1892

C. F. Titford died 23rd April 1899

E. M. J. Titford died 4th March 1902

B. J. Titford died 8th September 1905

W. Titford died 4th March 1918

If you're lucky, handwritten notes made by earlier generations of your family will have survived.

18

home and abroad, but that the milkman fell off his dray one day when he was drunk.

◆ Preparatory reading

Beyond your own family treasures, of course, lies the vast world of public records of one sort and another, but before you turn your attention to these, you would do well to read one or two of the basic guides to tracing your ancestry which have appeared in print over the last few decades, such as the evergreen *Beginning Your Family History* by George Pelling (8th edition, 2001). For a more detailed treatment of the subject you might like to refer to *Tracing Your Family Tree* by Jean Cole and John Titford (4th edition 2003), and at a stage when you feel you need to study the subject in even greater depth, you'll find *Ancestral Trails* by Mark Herber (revised edition 2003) indispensable.

Do think seriously about subscribing to certain relevant journals or magazines such as *The Genealogists' Magazine* (Society of Genealogists), *Family History* (Institute of Heraldic and Genealogical Studies), *Family History News and Digest* (Federation of Family History Societies), *Family Tree Magazine*, *Family History Monthly* and various journals published by Family History Societies.

Don't forget that there is a very close relationship between family history research and local history research. Local historians, when all is said and done, refer to much the same source material as family historians much of the time, though the use they make of their findings has a different emphasis. Look, then, at guides for local historians such as *Starting Out in Local History* by Simon Fowler (2001), *Sources for English Local History* by W. B. Stephens (3rd edition, Phillimore, 1994), *A Companion to Local History Research* by John Campbell-Kease (A. & C. Black, 1989) and especially *The Parish Chest* by W.E. Tate (2nd edition, Phillimore, 1983).

◆ Primary sources

'Primary sources' is a term used to describe original records made by someone who – in theory, at least – knew the truth of what was going on at the time in question. We can think of them, if you like, as being like water straight from the spring – as pure and unadulterated as we are likely to get in an imperfect world. Examples include: civil registration records of births, marriages and deaths; census returns; parish registers; bishops' transcripts; marriage allegations and bonds; non-parochial records; wills, administrations and other probate records; parish records; poor law records; diocesan records; borough or town records; quarter sessions records; other legal records; tax records; manorial records; newspapers; military records; records of the professions; guild and freedom records; various records of non-conformity; enclosure awards; tithe awards – and even monumental inscriptions. And that's just a start!

Original source material of this sort – or what you may take to be reliable transcripts made from it – will be your main port of call when it comes to building up a picture of the lives of your ancestors, the 'foreground' of your story, as I have called it, though it will often have relevance, if you examine it closely, to the broader historical background, too. It may well take you a great deal of effort, skill and time – years, even – to unearth this kind of detail, which is why family historians, once hooked, are never at a loss for something new to do.

COLLECTING MATERIAL: THE BACKGROUND

The process of trawling through primary source material in search of ancestors has probably taught you to focus very tightly. The trick has been to spot the names of family members as they lie hidden within a morass of archival material.

Now is the time to broaden that focus. A family history, after all, is very different from a mere pedigree or a list of facts about your ancestors. We're looking, ideally, for a story which sets the lives of those ancestors within a wider historical context.

Men and women in medieval times believed that they were living in a geocentric universe – that is, one that had the earth at its centre. The earth itself was set within a series of concentric spheres – each one invisible, of course – to which various heavenly bodies were attached. The universe, in other words, had more than a passing resemblance to an onion.

THE CHILDREN
OF
Jonah & Elizabeth Reeve,

Married March 18th, 1773.

ELIZABETH REEVE, *Mrs Worsley*
  Born 10th January, 1774, at 10 in the morning.
SARAH REEVE, *Mrs Unwin*
  Born 23rd November, 1775, at 11 at night.
MARY REEVE, *Mrs Vial*
  Born 23rd May, 1777, at 11 at night.
REBECCA REEVE, *Mrs Jerling*
  Born 28th October, 1778, at 3 in the morning.
JOSEPH REEVE,
  Born 14th May, 1780, at 9 in the evening.
RUTH ANN REEVE, *Mrs Bell*
  Born 19th June, 1782, at 5 in the morning.
THOMAS HOUSTON REEVE,
  Born 10th June, 1784, at 4 in the morning.
HEPHZIBAH REEVE, *Mrs Cooper*
  Born 7th December, 1785, at 3 in the morning.
SOPHIA REEVE,
  Born 22nd February, 1788, at 4 in the morning.
  (Died September, same year.)
WILLIAM BECKWITH REEVE,
  Born 3rd of July, 1789, at 3 in the morning.
JOHN FOSTER REEVE,
  Born 3rd July, 1790, at 5 in the morning.
SAMUEL HOUSTON REEVE,
  Born 25th August, 1795, at 6 in the morning.
SOPHIA REEVE, *Mrs Bright*
  Born 19th January, 1798, at 1 in the morning.

In rare instances, someone may even have gone to the trouble of producing a printed list of events relating to your family. Here are the children of Jonah Reeve of Bocking in Essex and his wife Elizabeth (née Houston) of St Helen's, Bishopsgate, who were married by licence at St Helen's in 1773.

This image will help us here, I hope. We could think of each of our ancestors as being like the earth in the geocentric system: around each person existed a system of contexts or environments within which a life had to be led. The individual lived within the context of his or her immediate family; that family operated within the context of an extended family; the extended family may have lived within a street or a lane; the street or lane probably lay within a hamlet, a village, a town, or a city; beyond that would be a county or a region, then a nation, then a continent, then the world as a whole. Every one of these contexts could affect our ancestor's thoughts and beliefs, his emotions, his actions, his choices – or the lack of them. The closer the context, the more powerful would be its influence – so the day-to-day affairs of your immediate family would usually impinge upon you more than would the more remote contexts. Usually, but not always – as great grandfather would have found out when he received his call-up papers and was whisked off to some remote battlefield during the First World War.

Use these contexts both to explain the actions of your ancestors, and to give the story of your family some substance. Work on the assumption that no man is an island.

It wouldn't be far from the truth to say that many of our ancestors were victims of one sort or another. Most of them were victims of the apprenticeship system, whereby a man would need to spend a specific number of years learning a trade; once learned, the trade might then earn a man his living, but it might prove difficult if not impossible to change his occupation in later years. Most people of modest means were victims of the settlement laws; if you strayed across the country, with or without your family, in search of work or a new home, be sure that the parish officials in your new parish would find you out soon enough. Unless you could fulfil certain criteria laid down by the settlement laws, or produce a settlement certificate, they would send you packing – back to your original parish of settlement by virtue of a removal order.

Victims, then. Our ancestors were also answerable for their actions in ways that we might find intolerable. To begin with, there were the neighbours. Only in Australian soap operas are neighbours quite so pleasant to each other so much of the time. In

Did your ancestors emigrate? Try to tell the story of their journey to a new home. ('Emigrants by the ship Ganges *departing for Canada', from* The Illustrated London News, *7 May 1870.)*

earlier centuries in England and elsewhere people could find themselves living cheek-by-jowl with some fairly objectionable people, nosey, censorious, interfering – violent, even.

There may have been few enough chances to escape the pressure – no car or public transport to take you to the nearest town to visit the shops or entertainment centres, no package

To the Constable of *Thwaite* and to all other Constables in the said County to execute.

WHEREAS *Mary Bernard* *Singlewoman* of the Parish *of Thwaite* in the County of *Norfolk* hath by her own voluntary Examination, taken in Writing upon Oath, before *us two* _____ of his Majesty's Justices of the Peace in and for the said County, this present Day declared herself to be with Child, and that the said Child or Children of which she now goeth is or are likely to be born in Bastardy, and to be chargeable to the Parish of *Thwaite* aforesaid, and that *George Hudson* of *Aylmerton* _____ in the said County, *Husbandman* did beget her with Child of the said Child or Children of which she now goeth.

AND whereas *John Wooley, Constable of Thwaite aforesaid* in order to indemnify the said Parish in the premises, hath applied to *us* to issue out *our* Warrant for the apprehending of the said *George Hudson* _____ We do therefore hereby command you immediately to apprehend the said *George Hudson* and to bring him before *us* or some other of his Majesty's Justices of the Peace for the said County, to find security to indemnify the said Parish of *Thwaite* _____ or else to find sufficient Security for his Appearance at the next General Quarter Sessions of the Peace to be holden for the said County, and to abide and perform such Order or Orders as shall be made, in pursuance of an Act passed in the Eighteenth Year of the Reign of her late Majesty, Queen Elizabeth, concerning Bastards begotten and born out of lawful Matrimony.

GIVEN under *our* Hands and Seals the *first* Day of *June* in the Year of our Lord, 181*3*

[Warrant before Birth.]

Many of our ancestors were victims of the operation of the poor laws. George Hudson of Aylmerton, Norfolk, husbandman, is to be apprehended by warrant because he has fathered a bastard child on Mary Bernard of Thwaite. 1st June 1813.

holidays. Just the neighbours, day in, day out, year in, year out, snooping, criticising, reporting you to the authorities.

Above and beyond the neighbours lay a wide range of such authorities to whom you might be answerable, many of them taking great delight in a spot of legalised snooping and keen to slap miscreants back into line. People were victims, again, then, as they found themselves answerable to the officers of the parish, to the archdeacon, the bishop, the manor courts, the hundred courts, quarter sessions – and a whole host of other law courts. Our ancestors' lives like ours, you may say, were circumscribed, as were the choices they were free to make. Their needs were simple enough – food, clothing, shelter, employment – but they also needed a spot of excitement or variety from time to time.

If you can, then, use the contexts within which your ancestors lived to flesh out the story you tell; consider in what way they were victims, and consider the authorities to which they were answerable. If your ancestors made a geographical move (despite the settlement laws), be it to the next village or even to another country, this will add spice and variety to your story. Did they also make significant social or economic moves, up or down the scale? All of this is grist to your story-telling mill!

A focused programme of background reading should stand you in good stead here, and will make you feel more of a 'proper' historian. A study of printed diaries or journals may really bring a period alive for you and could be used directly or indirectly in your narrative. Samuel Pepys and John Evelyn are classic diarists for the 17th century, James Woodforde for the 18th century and Francis Kilvert for the 19th. Don't forget, too, that imaginative literature such as novels often contains some wonderful period detail.

ORGANISING AND ARRANGING MATERIAL

With luck, then, you'll have no shortage of material as a basis for compiling your family history. You may feel that you have too little or too much information, in which case there will still be time to add to it or to subtract from it as you proceed.

We'd be wise, I think, to work on the assumption that you have more chance of achieving your goal if you know what that goal is before you start. At the outset, then, there are two questions you must ask yourself before you begin to organise your material ready to start writing.

DECISIONS

◆ *Which line of ancestry will you follow?*

You could be brave – or foolhardy – enough to attempt to write a story that encompasses all your known ancestors on every male and female line. What a pickle you could get yourself into! Better by far to stick to one ancestral line; you may well want to feature a male line which perpetuates the same surname, though wives who marry into the family will form part of the story, and their ancestry can be mentioned either in the main text or in footnotes or endnotes.

The surname you feature needn't be your own surname or maiden name, of course; you could start with your great grandmother's maiden name and follow that surname back as far as it will go. Many a very lively and convincing family history has been written in this way. Indeed, there's nothing to stop you writing a family history based upon your husband's or wife's ancestry or that of your best friend.

One further decision will need to be made at some point: even if you decide that you will write about the Pilkington family or some such, you will still have to choose between a number of options. Will this be your own branch of the Pilkingtons and none other – or will you have at least something to say about all the groupings of Pilkingtons you can find? You may only come up with an answer to this question as you go along, having thought through the implications of the different approaches. Don't delay the decision too long, for all that.

◆ *Writing the story: forwards or backwards?*

Will you write a chronological account of the family's history starting at some point in the past, or will you give an account of the way in which you conducted your research, working backwards in time from the present as each generation is discovered?

What intrigues and fascinates most family historians above everything else is the research process itself – the way that layer after layer of generations is peeled off, each one revealing the one beneath. You may well have surmounted what seemed like insuperable difficulties; you may have used lateral thinking, delved into scarcely-used original records or made earth-shattering discoveries by virtue of a lot of hard work or even thanks to a great stroke of luck. You may well feel that an account of your researches, taking the reader with you as you face the challenge of moving backwards and sideways through a steadily-growing pedigree, would make much more fascinating reading than a simple narrative account of the family's history. I still think that one of the best models to follow if you wish to write such an account is the book by Don Steel, *Discovering your Family History* (1980), written to accompany the excellent series of BBC television programmes which featured Gordon Honey-combe's quest for his ancestry.

If you decide to write a narrative account, you'll have to put your brain in reverse, as it were. A story which you researched backwards in time from the present day, one generation at a time into the past, will then need to be told forwards in time as a narrative, starting with the earliest significant date. If you have traced your ancestors back through the records of civil registration in England and Wales, Scotland or Ireland, from a person's marriage to his or her birth and so on, it's almost tempting at times to believe that your ancestors lived their lives in this way.

◆ *Arranging your material in a chronological sequence*

Your initial decisions have been made, then? If you choose to write your story backwards, by way of a 'How I did it' account, you could have a lot of fun. It would be unwise to try to formulate definitive rules governing the exact contents or arrangement of such a book; just try to make it gripping, don't give away too much at once, and provide plenty of illustrations. Some of what follows in this book may be useful and relevant to you, but from now on we will focus more precisely on the other option mentioned, a narrative account of a family's history, the alternative most commonly adopted.

The Happy Event
took place at
Royal Northern Hospital

Holloway, N7.
on Sunday, January 21st 1945.

Doctor Mr. Lane - Roberts.

Nurse Bradshaw.

Did someone in your family purchase a blank book of the 'Baby's days' variety, and fill in details?

If you've been assiduous in collecting material relevant to your chosen family and have been working away at such a project for quite a long while, you will no doubt have arranged your notes in some kind of order. I do hope so! If you haven't been so organised, the task of preparing the ground for writing a family history will take that much longer to complete.

What might you have done? Perhaps you have a series of files, or computer files, headed Wills, Census Returns and Civil Registration Records? If you've discovered a batch of family members in a particular set of parish registers, you may have entered all relevant entries under the headings of Baptisms, Marriages and Burials. That's fine for keeping your own records neat and tidy, but you can't sit down and write a family history straight from notes organised in this way. Real life isn't and wasn't like this; a person would be baptised, then married, then buried. He or she might appear in census or other records, and may have left a will. In other words, the chronology of a person's life would hop around, in and out of your carefully classified records.

What you need – and if your own experience proves that this is not the case, congratulations! – is a single chronological listing of events which are relevant to your family. From such a list you can then start your story without much difficulty. Ideally your listing would be made with the use of a computer; if not, you can use index cards or sheets of paper fixed into one or more loose-leaf binders.

Start with any record you choose, not necessarily the earliest one. The first one to hand could be the marriage of William Good to Agnes Peabody in Kendal, Westmorland, on 23 June 1798. Write or type '1798' at the head of the page, then enter the information. You may want to record simply a brief summary of an event, cross-referencing the entry to the fuller details in your main files. When you come to another event which took place in 1798, enter this on the same page; if not, start a new page.

Perhaps you can see why a computer is ideal for this task? Your growing chronological list should not be restricted to family details alone; enter events of local, national, and even international importance. Note that life in the family village was affected by an enclosure award, a series of bad harvests or an outbreak of cholera in that year; refer to the death of Oliver Cromwell or the accession of King Charles II; mention the fact that the English were busy losing the American colonies at that time – and so on. You will steadily be creating a genuine chronology of events in which births, marriages, deaths, census returns, wills, and national and international events will be mixed up together – exactly as they happened in the real world to real people.

This might sound like a laborious process to undertake, just when you're keen to start writing your story, but it pays dividends in the long run, believe me. You will have the bare bones of your story mapped out before you start. Not only that, but you may well notice connections which had previously escaped you. You might realise that a very large number of family members were buried in different parts of the country in a certain year; was there a national epidemic? You might realise that a certain lady got married very soon after the death of her widowed father; had she been nursing him through his final illness, feeling free to marry only once he had died? You might notice that a married couple have children every two years or so, but that there is a then a six-year gap during the early years of the 19th century; was the husband away fighting against Napoleon?

Organising your material under a series of classified headings, then, is fine for everyday use, but will probably not help you when you come to write a narrative, unless you can hold a very wide range of information in your head at one time.

◆ A pedigree chart

What you will also need is some kind of pedigree chart to help you organise your thoughts; most people's minds can grasp the intricacies of a family's relationships much more clearly if it is presented in this visual form. I've always found it easiest to make sense of what is called a 'drop-line' family tree: that is, one which features the earliest-known ancestor at the top, with each generation 'dropped down' the page vertically. A marriage is indicated by an equals sign (=), and a short vertical line coming down from a married couple then meets a horizontal line at right angles, along which the children are placed. Most people start at the left with the eldest child, then work along to the right, but sometimes you'll find all the males grouped together on the left, in order of birth, followed by all the females.

◆ Sections, chapters and cameos

If you start writing a family story, ploughing on until you've finished and then simply stop, you'll have a very strange piece of work on your hands. Your text needs to be organised and arranged in a logical way, if only for the sake of that potentially-bewildered readership of yours.

We can think of the narrative you write in terms of small and large units. Letters make up words, words make up sentences, sentences make up paragraphs, paragraphs make up what we might call 'sections' (each, ideally, with its own section title or heading), sections make up chapters (also bearing some kind of title), and eventually chapters can be joined together to make up a fully-fledged book. A further refinement you might like to consider is to group various chapters together into larger units which you might refer to as 'parts' (the Smiths of Appleby, the Smiths of Whitehaven and the Smiths of Workington).

Chapters are essential building-blocks in this process, but there is no reason why you should not think of each one as a kind of 'cameo', a bite-size chunk complete in itself and quite capable of standing alone if necessary. Write a cameo and see how it goes. Give it – or sell it? – to those who might find it interesting, and get some feedback. Feature it on the Internet if you like, give a copy to a library or to a Family History Society, or get it published in a relevant magazine. Write another cameo – and another – and see if you end up with a complete book at the end of it.

One advantage of what we might refer to as a 'modular' approach such as this is that there is no reason why you should compose such cameos in strict chronological order. By all means write an 18th century cameo first, followed by one set in the 17th century, then feature the 19th or 20th centuries.

Think in terms of cameos, then. What will give each of these a coherence and a focus? Such a question leads us on to a vital consideration, another decision to make in the early stages of your great project.

◆ *Concurrent or consecutive lives?*

Will each of your cameos feature an account of concurrent or consecutive lives? In other words, will you lump together several individuals that make up a family group in one single cameo, or will you separate them out, taking each person one at a time?

The fact is, of course, that the lives of several individuals in your story will overlap in time. Any given decade, for example, may be lived through by brothers and sisters, their parents, their uncles and aunts, their grandparents, their grand uncles and aunts – even their great grandparents and great grand uncles and aunts.

The decision you must make without delay is this: will you write one chapter featuring, say, a pair of brothers called Fred and George together – or will you write a chapter on Fred, and then a separate chapter on George? On balance I favour the latter. If you tell the story of Fred and George together, that is, concurrently, you'll probably end up leap-frogging your way through the narrative. You may take Fred from birth to marriage, then on to early parenthood in a different town; then you'll find yourself writing something like, 'Meanwhile, back at the ranch ... when we last met George he was a babe in arms . . .' and you'll take George into middle age before picking up Fred again and letting him overtake George. This can get very messy and confusing. The one danger you must face if you tell the story consecutively (Fred, then George), however, is that you'll probably be covering much of the same period of time, and must avoid repetition.

This distinction between a concurrent/consecutive approach to writing a narrative is one that may not have occurred to you – but, believe me, it can be of crucial importance. It's perhaps the single most vital aspect of writing a family history that I wish I'd thought about more carefully before I wrote my own book on the Titford family. Had I done so, I could have saved myself hours of wasted work and a great deal of anguish.

When I wrote the story of my own family, I decided in the end to use the 'consecutive' option exclusively. I followed my own direct line of ancestry and compiled one chapter for each adult male in each generation – of whom there were never very many, luckily for me! Every chapter took the man's name as its title,

NEWCASTLE
UPON TYNE. } ff.

YOU fwear, That you fhall from henceforth hold with our Sovereign *Lord* ——— the *King's* Majefty that now is, and with *his* Heirs and Succeffors, Kings and Queens of *Great Britain*, againft all Perfons, to live and to die, and maintain the Peace and all the Franchifes of this Town of *Newcaftle upon Tyne*, and be obedient to the MAYOR, ALDERMEN, SHERIFF, and all other the Officers of the fame, and their Counfel keep; and no Man's Goods avow for yours, unlefs he be as free as yourfelf, and of the fame Franchife : And you fhall obferve and keep to the beft of your Power, all lawful Ordinances made by common Confent, on High Court-days; and all other Things you fhall do that belong to a FREEMAN of the faid Town.

So help you GOD.

FORTITER DEFENDIT TRIUMPHANS.

Chriftopher Fawcett Efquire was —— this fourth —— Day of November in —— the Year of our Lord God 1771 admitted —— a free Burgefs of this Corporation, before the Right Worfhipfull Sir Walter Blackett Bart Mayor and ftands charged with a Mufket for the Defence thereof.

Gibfon

Wr Blackett, Mayor

Various boroughs admitted freemen, and an attractive certificate could be the result. Christopher Fawcett was admitted as a free burgess of Newcastle upon Tyne on 4th November 1771.

complete with some distinguishing nickname which I had invented for him wherever necessary – so I had chapters with titles like Charles Frederick, Thomas the Alehousekeeper, Ralph the Pauper, Thomas the Calvinist, Charles the Cheesemonger, and so on. Because I hoped to relate each man's life to a period of history, I also used a sub-title for each chapter: The Civil War, Poverty in the Countryside, The French Threat. You can work on the assumption that at least one brother or sister in each generation will be an interesting or unusual character, or that something interesting or unusual will have happened to him or her – which is almost the same thing.

Do also think about what a person did not do, as well as what he or she did. Why did great aunt Agnes never get married? Why didn't grandfather fight in the Second World War? Why did your ancestor not emigrate to Canada with both his brothers? Why wasn't great uncle Fred apprenticed to a tailor, when all the other boys were?

Perhaps one day you will stumble across a trunk full of family papers, some of which could be used to illustrate your family history. A mouth-watering thought! This illustration first appeared in a sale catalogue published by Dominic Winter Book Auctions, Swindon, in March 1999.

WRITING YOUR FAMILY HISTORY

Please can I start writing my story now? I hear you say. Almost now, I reply. First, a word of warning. Whatever you do, don't be too ambitious in what you set out to achieve. Aim to write a succinct story; if it grows as you go along, that's fine, but don't set yourself an impossible task at the beginning. The world is full of unfinished PhD theses. Many a student on a PhD course spends the first year gathering information far and wide, planning a thesis which is totally unrealistic in scope; the second year might then be spent in total despair, and the third in planning an exquisite and suitable suicide. Be warned – keep it manageable from the outset!

So. You've seized the day and rejected all excuses. Your decisions have been made. You've done your research and some background reading. You know which ancestral line you will follow. You know whether you will tell the story forwards or backwards. You've prepared a chronological set of notes on your family's affairs set within a framework of local and national events, and you have a pedigree to work from. You'll tackle the overall project in terms of smaller units such as cameos. You've decided whether to feature concurrent or consecutive lives.

You are now like a decorator who has carried out the laborious preparation necessary before the real job begins – you've stripped the window-frames of old paint and slapped on a coat of primer. You are now ready to dip your brush into the can of gloss paint – the really creative stage has arrived.

I shall now delay you only long enough to suggest that there are two more decisions to make at this point, and these have to do with the writing process itself, rather than the planning stage, which is now safely behind us. After that, you'll be relieved to hear, you can start writing in earnest.

DECISIONS

◆ *Who exactly are you writing the family story for?*

Who are your intended readers? Are they members of your family? Other family historians? Historians in general? The world? Do try to be more specific than simply 'the general public'.

In the days when I was a teacher of communication studies, we used to talk about an 'awareness of audience'. That is, having decided upon your intended readership or audience, keep that audience constantly in mind as you write. Any piece of communication can only be judged to be good or bad, effective or ineffective, in terms of what it aims to do and who it aims to do it for. Do you aim to inform, educate and entertain? Only one or two of these, or all three?

As to audience, if you write for your immediate family, you can relax – even share a few in-jokes with them; if you write for a broader readership, you may choose to be slightly more formal.

How much do you assume that your readers already know about the arcane world of family history research? Have they heard of the Hearth Tax, do they understand the importance of Hardwicke's Marriage Act, do they know what a Settlement Certificate was? If you write a statement like this :

I found great-great grandfather in the B.T.s, living in a peculiar

are your readers to suppose that he was a full-blown alcoholic, shacked up in some kind of commune?

Above all you should try to achieve an empathy with your readers – that is, try to feel what it is like for them to read your story when they don't have the knowledge that you have, and, worse, may not share your passionate interest in the whole thing. Assume that they need to be won over, persuaded, by your infectious enthusiasm. Don't bore them to death, don't try to impress them with your erudition – but don't patronise them and assume that they know nothing whatever. And, yes, if in doubt, do tell them all about the Hearth Tax, about Hardwicke and about a Settlement Certificate; if they already know, they'll feel very pleased with themselves, and if they don't know, they'll be glad of the clarification.

◆ *Will you write as a story teller, or as a historian?*

I am grateful to Terrick Fitzhugh's excellent book, *How To Write a Family History* (1988), for drawing to my attention the important distinction between the approaches taken by a 'story teller' and a 'historian'. What is that distinction? The historian is apt to make historical judgements as he goes along – indeed, he would regard it as one of his primary functions to do so. Will you make value judgements as you tell the story of your ancestors? Will you criticise your male ancestors for their treatment of women? Will you castigate your forebears for galloping across the countryside in pursuit of a fox, for eating red meat, for not being concerned about the fate of the rainforests or the world's stock of whales?

Someone once said that it's easy to have 20-20 vision in retrospect. We can all make supercilious judgements after the event, with the wisdom of hindsight. What, after all, will our descendants make of us? The past, they say, is a different country – and so it is. Why not spare our ancestors the spotlight of anything approaching political correctness and its bedfellow, righteous indignation? Perhaps we have to accept that most of our forebears led their lives to the best of their ability, given the constraints of the historical period in which they lived?

My own view is that it isn't helpful to make retrospective judgements on our ancestors, that we should accompany them on their journey through life, walk with them down the tunnel which constituted their existence, not knowing where it might lead or whether there would be light at the end or not. Share with them their ignorance as well as their knowledge. They may well not have known or suspected that war was about to break out, that the plague was soon to erupt, that they would lose five children in infancy. Just as you would aim to have empathy with the readers of your book, have empathy with your ancestors, too.

200 Hermitage Road
Finsbury Park
N 4

My dear Nephew
            Your Cousin Emily & myself
are very sorry to hear the sad news of
the loss of your dear Mother
and offer you & your Brothers & Sister
our deep sympathy in your bereavement-
she has been a great sufferer but now
she is at rest & away from all pain
& sorrow may God give you wisdom
& strength to discharge all things
right in his sight—

            God bless you all

            Yours affectionately
                        Uncle Walter

I feel I would like to go to the Funeral
so will be at the House at 2/o
on Monday

A bereavement would often generate correspondence which may have survived in a family archive. Typically there might be a 'loving memory' card (below) and/or a related letter of condolence (left).

A loving mother, true and kind,
She was to us in heart and mind;
A careful one, who loved us well,
When she on earth with us did dwell.

In Affectionate Remembrance of

Mary Ann Titford,

Who departed this life Dec. 3rd, 1930

Aged 80 Years

And was Interred at Abney Park Cemetery
Dec. 8th   Grave No. 62076

17 Freegrove Road,
N. 7.

38

A FUNNY OLD BUSINESS

Let writing commence. To use an oxymoron, this is where the 'satisfying slog' begins.

To begin with, you may find that your creative energy – and you will certainly have some! – comes in fits and starts. Some days you will sit down to write and the words just won't come out in the right way. You can't turn fluency on like a tap, and if you're tired, or your mind is on other things, there'll be days when you creak your way through the writing process. There are two views on all this, and I won't be prescriptive about which you will find most convincing. There are those who say that you should be disciplined in your approach, forcing yourself to sit down and write, say, for an hour each day, for a two-hour slot each week, or whatever. Others will maintain that there is little point in hitting your head against a brick wall if the words just won't come; leave it for a while, wait until the creative muse is on top form, and sit down for a writing session whenever you feel the urge.

Whichever of these strategies you adopt, you really do need to be disciplined to some degree if you are ever to finish your task. Set yourself an overall deadline ('I will have finished this family history two years from now') and, if you can, short-term deadlines as well ('I will have written two cameos by the end of next month'). Deadlines – and they should be realistic deadlines – focus the mind wonderfully; they will sometimes force you to keep going even when you don't much feel like it (not always a bad thing) and they will probably persuade you that you'll simply have to leave some things out of your story – that is, to edit. Also no bad thing! Some people work well under pressure, others don't, but you must put at least some pressure on yourself if you are to write your family history. If you don't, then Parkinson's Law will operate, your time will be filled up with other things, and you'll get nowhere. There will always be some task or other which you will have to lay aside if you are to do some serious writing.

If you allow everyday life to crowd out your writing time, then rest assured that it will do just that. You may even find that the time you spend being creative as a writer puts a certain amount of strain upon your relationship with your own family – which is why a number of books carry a dedication to the author's husband, wife and/or children 'for their patience and understanding while this book was being written'. It's really a matter of balance, isn't it? No point in breaking your own present-day family asunder just to write a story of what your family got up to in the past!

So, I repeat, writing a book is a funny old business. You may even find that male authors will tell you that bringing their book to completion is the nearest thing a man can ever get to having a baby! Indeed, there are similarities – especially when, after months of patient work, it seems at times as if the book will never be finished, the birth will never happen. To me, one of the most aggravating things about writing a book occurs at the stage when I really do think that I've almost finished, that only a few things remain to be done. Just the introduction to write, the bibliography to compile, the illustrations to be chosen and captioned, the final proof-reading to be done, and so on. Maybe by that stage I've exhausted myself or allowed my creative energy to run low, but the last steps in the process of bringing a book to completion can be the most frustrating. Don't let me put you off; it may not be like that for you!

One other thing will probably happen to you: your subconscious mind will be churning away a lot of the time, thinking about what you've already written and what you intend to write next. Flashes of inspiration may come to you when you're driving the car, digging the garden, hanging out the washing, listening to a sermon or watching television. Don't let such flashes sink down again into the nether regions; jot down a few notes on a piece of paper for future use – or use a small hand held tape recorder. If the bug really bites you, you might even wake up in the middle of the night and find yourself scrawling a note or two in case you've forgotten it by morning.

If stray ideas come to me while I'm busy typing the main text itself onto the computer, I very often skip to the end of the document I'm working on, make a few notes, and then return to where I was before.

Now, as a writer, you're on your own – in more ways than one. You'll probably need to find a quiet corner in which you can just sit and be madly creative, a place where you can spread books and papers all over the desk – and on the floor, of course – without anyone complaining too much. But you're on your own in another way – that is, no one can tell you how to write as such. Teachers or helpful friends could give you a few hints regarding good style, could help out in specific matters of grammar, spelling and punctuation, but you will need to write in your own way – ideally in a manner which allows your own personality and view of the world to emerge. Do try to relax, to be yourself. I once had a car which never seemed to want to go into reverse gear; the more I tried to force the gear lever, the worse things became. The only way to persuade the lever into reverse was to make a conscious effort to relax, to stop tensing the muscles. Then it went in like a dream. And so it is with writing: it's possible to try too hard, to strain every brain cell to the point where you can either write nothing at all, or what you do write seems stilted and strained. Try to relax as you write, enjoy yourself, take it easy, use a touch of humour and wit (without being flippant), try to entertain your readers, be bright, enthusiastic.

When it comes to the quality of your writing, there is a catch – a 'Catch 22', even. It works like this: the better you become at writing (and rest assured that you will, as time goes on), the higher the standards you will then set yourself for the future. This is one of life's little cruelties, you might say, in this as in so many other fields of human activity. In other words, you can't win ...

NUTS AND BOLTS

I was once an English teacher, so without much prompting I could bore for England on the subject of grammar, spelling and punctuation. I'll spare you most of that, suggesting instead that you refer to one of the many manuals on such subjects which can be picked up at a modest price at any bookshop worthy of the name. For now, here are a few basic hints to get you started:

◆ *Grammar*

Choose a fairly simple and straightforward manual dealing with grammar or 'English usage' and read it carefully, but refuse to be intimidated by it. You'll learn about such matters as whether you should begin a sentence with a conjunction (whyever not?) or end it with a preposition. You'll discover how to distinguish between 'fewer' and 'less', and between 'imply' and 'infer'. You'll find out all about split infinitives ('to boldly go') and the use of the subjunctive, and be told that to write a sentence such as 'He wrote a letter to my husband and I' or 'Cycling along the road, the car knocked him over' (the dreaded 'hung participle') constitutes a hanging offence. Not so many years ago, stuff like this was being taught to school children at quite a young age – but times have moved on ...

What about these and similar rules, then? Follow them if you can, but don't get at all paranoid about them, and break any rule if the alternative is to write a piece of ugly and convoluted English.

◆ *Punctuation*

Plenty of tripe and nonsense has been written on this subject, but don't take it all very seriously. Good punctuation should have one aim above all others – to make it easier for a reader to follow what you've written without backtracking or having to puzzle over obscure or ambiguous passages of writing.

Many a teacher would tell you (and maybe one did tell you once upon a time?) that in an ideal world you would make use of a variety of sentences – short ones and longer complex ones. That's fine if you're happy with it, but my more down-to-earth recommendation would be that, if in doubt, you should say what you have to say, finish off your sentence with a full-stop, then start a new sentence.

I am a great fan of the semi-colon, however, as you may have noticed in my own writing. Semi-colons are wonderful things – somewhere between a comma and a full-stop, they allow you to hold one statement in abeyance while you add another one to it. Experiment with them if you like; you probably haven't developed your full potential as a writer unless you've played around with the ubiquitous semi-colon.

And ... (notice the conjunction) you won't forget to use

paragraphs, will you? If a sentence contains one basic idea, expanded or not as the case may be, then a paragraph contains a related set of such ideas. One topic, if you like.

◆ *Spelling*

Generally you've either got this, or you haven't. I have many very intelligent and highly-educated friends whose spelling is abysmal. Or rather, they habitually misspell twenty or so key words. Use a dictionary by all means – though you do need to know at least something about the spelling of a word in order to find it in a dictionary at all! Try to remember that *practise* spelt with an 's' is a verb, while *practice* spelt with a 'c' is a noun. The same is true of the words *license* and *licence*, despite what your local pub or Indian restaurant may think! And we all know about 'i' before 'e', except after 'c', don't we?

If you're using a word processor, you'll no doubt activate the spell-checker. This doesn't solve all problems, of course; some of the terms you'll use in a family history narrative will be unknown to the checker, and if you use the exact wording of an original document or two, the checker will want to 'correct' much of it. Unusual words, including names, which you use very frequently can usually be added to the checker's existing memory. Sometimes, of course, the spell-checker will give you some hilarious and way-off-the-mark alternatives, and if I type 'twelve pint type' instead of 'twelve point type', there will be no correction made, since 'pint' is a perfectly proper word in its own right. A spell-checker can perform some very clever functions, but it can't read your mind.

Now please bear with me while I offer you a series of further hints on some related topics:

◆ *Quotations*

You'll probably want to use quotations of one sort or another fairly frequently in a family history, and can separate then from the main text by using quotation marks or by featuring them in a distinguishing type-face such as italics.

If you've tape-recorded your aunt's reminiscences, why try to re-phrase what she said in your own words? Let her speak for herself! Quote her exact words, indicating those passages you have omitted by the use of three dots in the text. Do have the courtesy, of course, to ask Auntie whether she has any objections to being featured in your family history in this way.

When it comes to including transcriptions of documents written in earlier centuries, the general rule is to quote the original text verbatim – unusual grammar, spelling, punctuation and all. I even transcribe *Ye* (meaning 'the') with a letter 'Y', even though I know that the 'Y' was just a corruption of an older similar letter-form called a thorn, representing a 'th' sound.

Incidentally, you won't be infringing copyright if you quote a short passage from a printed book, though you should acknowledge the source in a suitably detailed way.

◆ *Footnotes or endnotes*

If family historians are ever to be taken seriously in the wider world of historical research – and, goodness knows, many do deserve to be! – then they must get in the habit of quoting their sources. You will need to do this with precision. Which documents did you refer to? Are they in your own possession, or are they lodged in a record repository – and if so, which one? What are the relevant 'call numbers' or exact references? Present this information in the following form:

'Settlement Certificate, 10 March 1723/4. Somerset Record Office. SRO DD/LW/18'.

What printed material have you referred to? It may have been a pamphlet, or a book – in which case, give the name of the author, the precise title, the edition (if relevant), the publication date and the relevant page number(s), like this:

'Stephens, W.B. *Sources for English Local History*. 3rd Edition, 1994. p.63ff.'

Note in this case that 'p.63ff.' means: 'page 63 and the pages which immediately follow it', while 'pp.63, 64' would mean 'pages 63 and 64'. If relevant references to a particular topic or person occur throughout a published work, the term 'passim' is commonly used.

Use some scholarly bibliographical abbreviations when quoting your sources if you like – but it's not compulsory. I'm speaking here about little gems such as 'op. cit.' (from the Latin, *opere citato*), meaning 'in the work already quoted', or 'ibid' (from the Latin *ibidem*), meaning 'in the same book, chapter, passage, etc'. To get some idea as to how these work, look at the footnotes or end-notes to some serious historical publications, or have a close read of *Researching and Writing History: a practical guide for local historians* by David Dymond (2000).

We owe it to our readers to share information with them in this way, if only because, in theory at least, any interested researcher who reads what you have written can then refer back to your original source material if necessary and draw his or her own conclusions from it.

Heaven forbid that we should ever lay ourselves open to the charge levelled by Margaret Stuart, author of *Scottish Family History* (1978 reprint of a 1930 original) at those who write what she calls an 'anecdotal family history':

> *This is frequently the work of a lady. It lacks, as a rule, a sufficient number of dates and almost always lacks references.* (p. 16)

Phew! Avoid falling into such a category at all costs!

The most usual and effective way of defining your sources is to use footnotes or endnotes:

Footnotes. The very word suggests that these will appear at the foot of each page, which is indeed the case. To create a *footnote*, place a small number (use 'superscript' on a computer) at the end of the sentence in the main text to which it will refer, and place the footnote, preceded by the same number, at the bottom of the relevant page. Footnotes are usually presented in smaller-point type in order to distinguish them from the text itself.

Footnotes might be kind to readers much of the time, but they can be a nightmare for writers to organise, and you'll sometimes find that they spill over from the bottom of one page to the bottom of the next – a messy procedure.

Not only that, but I can vividly recall the experience of teaching Shakespeare using the splendid *Arden* edition of his plays, only to find that on some pages there were only three lines or so of

Shakespeare, supplemented by a footnote of monumental proportions compiled by the editor!

Endnotes. These work in a similar way, except that you don't place them at the foot of each page, but group them together at the end of a chapter or towards the back of the book itself.

My own advice, based upon some experience and experimentation, is to use endnotes. If you do so, you can happily add, subtract or re-number such notes at will, without throwing your page-by-page layout into chaos. I'd also recommend that you use a separate endnote numbering sequence for each chapter of your book, running from, say, '1' to '16' in the first chapter and then starting at '1' again for the second. This approach also makes it easier to make changes with minimum disruption. Whether you then decide to place the endnotes relating to chapter one immediately after the chapter itself, or save them all up to the end, is a matter of personal choice. Different authors favour different approaches, just as some decide to present a short bibliography ('further reading') after each chapter, and others save everything up for a final listing.

You can use footnotes or endnotes for more than simply quoting your sources, of course. Consider including some or all of the following:

Further family notes. It's important not to clog up your text with material which might be of interest to readers, but which is ultimately a side-issue that would interrupt the main flow of the narrative. Relegate such extra material to your notes (or to an appendix). Here you can, if you wish, say something about the ancestry of related or distaff lines – that is, those of women who marry into the main family with which you are dealing.

Conjecture. There will be times when you are still uncertain about some key facts or vital relationships. Henry's birth has not been registered, yet you assume that he is the eldest son of John. Then there seem to be two contemporary Thomases, probably father and son, and a number of references might relate to either man. What do you do? It's best to decide upon one possibility which you find most convincing, and to stick with this in your main text. Meanwhile, in your notes, say quite honestly that there is a degree of conjecture here, and explain what you are doing: 'For the purpose of the story, I have assumed that ... '. Don't keep on apologising for the same uncertainty! The general rule is never to use conjecture on any serious issue without noting the fact. It simply isn't fair to your readers or to yourself to present hypothesis or conjecture as fact.

THE CONTENT OF THE STORY

So much for some of the mechanics of good writing and of quoting your sources. What about the content you will feature using your finely-honed writing skills?

Above all, as you write, do try to get inside the skins of your ancestors – seek that empathy that allows you to share with them what they felt and thought, to experience with them their joys, frustrations, hopes and aspirations. If your research has been thorough and your pedigree is correct, then these people had at least some influence upon your own genetic make-up. Now is your chance to breathe new life back into them, to give their lives, however humble, a further touch of dignity and meaning. Let's hope that one day your descendants may do as much for you!

It will be obvious to most family history researchers that the further you go back in time, the less you will know about your ancestors. You may have stumbled across a 'gateway' ancestral link that takes you back through nobility to royalty, but that would be the exception rather than the rule. If you spring from humble or middling stock, you will probably know precious little about your 16th or 17th century ancestors – even if you have found out their names!

The trick here is this: the less you know about an ancestor, the more you feature the background when you tell his or her story. After all, the life of a person settled in a small village in centuries past will be inextricably linked with the history of the village itself. Small communities could be claustrophobic places in which everyone knew everyone else – and in which many villagers would be related by blood. So if you tell the story of the village you will in effect be telling the story of your ancestors.

If the foreground grows dim, bring up the background, as it were. Have something to say about the operation of the Elizabethan Poor Laws, about the life of a shoemaker, the tribulations of the English Civil War, the stigma of illegitimacy,

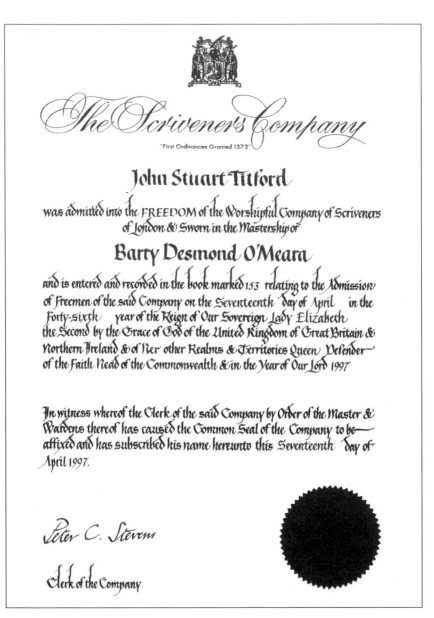

The Scrivener's Company

"First Ordinances Granted 1373"

John Stuart Titford

was admitted into the FREEDOM of the Worshipful Company of Scriveners of London & Sworn in the Mastership of

Barty Desmond O'Meara

and is entered and recorded in the book marked 153 relating to the Admission of Freemen of the said Company on the Seventeenth day of April in the Forty-sixth year of the Reign of Our Sovereign Lady Elizabeth the Second by the Grace of God of the United Kingdom of Great Britain & Northern Ireland & of Her other Realms & Territories Queen Defender of the Faith Head of the Commonwealth & in the Year of Our Lord 1997

In witness whereof the Clerk of the said Company by Order of the Master & Wardens thereof has caused the Common Seal of the Company to be affixed and has subscribed his name hereunto this Seventeenth day of April 1997.

Peter C. Stevens

Clerk of the Company

Will you include a brief account of your own life story in your family history book? Why not feature a few relevant documents from your files?

48

the price of food, the weather. This is where the time you may have been able to spend reading books on local or national history will pay great dividends.

For all that, beware of making bold statements such as 'The 1930s was a decade during which storm clouds were gathering ...' unless you can relate such a statement in some meaningful way to the lives of your ancestors. In cases like this, the well-known English genealogist, Michael Gandy, says that we should ask ourselves the question: 'Were those storm clouds gathering down your grandparents' street?' Michael goes even further, offering us a salutary reminder that 'Our ancestors led their lives slowly, day by day, as we do ... In real life there isn't a story. The future isn't waiting to happen. Most of it is unpredictable, because it's an accident ... '

I seem to have read a great number of family histories which fall all too easily into the 'great sweep of history' trap, and which say something like this:

The early nineteenth century saw a flowering of literary talent as the novels of Jane Austen and the work of the Romantic poets scaled new heights ...

True, true – but what effect might the literary world have had upon your own ancestors? Could they read? Were they sitting at home chatting about Wordsworth and Coleridge, or were they more concerned about the price of bread and the fact that the local pub had been damaged during a thunder storm?

You may have interests of your own, beyond family history as such, which will enable you to bring alive the milieu in which your ancestors lived, giving the reader a real feel for the texture of their everyday lives. You may know something about food in times past, or about music, transport, health or the weather. You may have read a good deal about certain trades or professions; why not reconstruct for the reader a typical day in the life of a blacksmith, a trawlerman, a country doctor or a parson? Costume may fascinate you, and you may be able to say something meaningful about what your ancestors wore, or probably wore. And how did your ancestors speak? Would they have used a strong regional dialect or accent – and if so, of what kind?

Always remember, too, that even when you know *what* an

ancestor did and *when* he did it, your judgement as to *why* he acted in the way he did can form part of the story. You may well have to use conjecture – but don't allow mere guesswork to stand in your text as fact. Suppose, if you like, that your ancestor supported Oliver Cromwell in the 1650s because he was ideologically committed to the parliamentary cause – but don't state it to be so unless you have real evidence. Maybe your man would always support the winning side, keen to get on with his everyday business?

As you approach the present day, you may well find that you know too much, not too little, about your ancestors and relations. You won't be able to include everything, and will have to edit. What a good discipline! Not only that, but some of the information you have may well be contradictory. Some people say that great aunt Ada was an adorable, cuddly old lady. Others maintain that she was a real harridan. Which is the truth? Was she one or the other, or a bit of both? It might be foolhardy to attempt a judgement of your own, so why not simply present the alternatives for the reader to think about?

EDITING AND REVISION

You'll be editing in two different ways as you proceed. To begin with, there's the family history material which will form the basis of your book, some of which you'll decide to use and some of which you'll have to reject, no matter how reluctantly. Don't include everything you know about your family just because you know it; if you do, you'll clog up your text and neither you nor the reader will be able to see the wood for the trees. Your accumulated family information is simply a source from which you will write your narrative; you'll have to be selective. Don't include material which is unduly tedious, repetitive or only peripheral to the main thrust of the story.

◆ *Skeletons*

You may want to think very carefully about whether you'll let skeletons out of their cupboards. You may feel that they should be let out, shaken, dusted down and included – if only because you're writing a family history, not building a family monument. It won't always be so simple, alas. You might think that unearthing a bit of scandal – illegitimacy or minor crime – is all part of life's rich tapestry, but there may be those still alive who had carefully kept the skeleton cupboard door closed and who would be quite genuinely (if unjustifiably?) upset if you were to include material which they regard as embarrassing or even shameful.

You do want to tell the truth, but you don't want to cause offence. If you can, talk it all through with anyone who might be worried, to see if you can come to some compromise. If not, try to gauge the depth of feeling you're encountering and act accordingly. Is it worth causing deep offence to a close relation for the sake of writing a book that pulls no punches?

◆ *Editing and revising the text*

So you'll need to edit your raw material, deciding what goes in and what stays out. Not only that, but once you've started writing you'll also need to edit or revise your text. If you were a genius beyond measure, you'd simply sit down, write a book from start to finish, stop, and publish. Alas, for us lesser mortals life isn't quite like that. You really will have to undertake a certain amount of editing and revision of some sort – not root and branch, we hope, but significant for all that.

My own favoured way of proceeding is as follows: I write a certain amount of text – a chapter or a section, possibly – and I leave it for a few days at least, maybe longer. Then I return to it and make revisions as necessary. I'll correct spelling or punctuation errors, I'll re-phrase sentences that sound clumsy or where the meaning isn't clear. I may cut out whole paragraphs or even pages because I don't think they're necessary any more, and I may rearrange other blocks of text. You can see why a word processor is so vital if you want to do this job swiftly and efficiently! There was a time when I would have used off-cuts of paper and a pot of glue. Perish the thought!

You really can't afford to be too precious about everything you've written. Even if you sweated blood to complete a page or two of text, you must be brutal at the revision stage if you decide that it isn't so vital or interesting after all. The more you prune your text, the stronger it will be. To change the metaphor: I always say that it's easier to cut dead flesh than living flesh. The moment after you've finished writing a page or two, nothing would persuade you to abandon it or to edit it severely. Two weeks later you can perhaps take a more detached view. Yes, you thought it was good at the time, it cost you a great deal of energy to write it, it was once precious to you – but now it must be brutally cut. The writer's waste-paper basket, like the film editor's cutting room floor, will eventually fill up with all sorts of wonderful material that somehow failed to make it into the final version.

If you don't mind laying yourself open to constructive criticism, you might be brave enough to ask a friend or relation, or both, to give you an opinion of a sample of your book as it develops. Hand over a section, a cameo or a chapter to people whose judgment you trust, and ask for an honest opinion. Is the information accurate? Has anything been missed out? Does the narrative make sense? Does the style of writing seem appropriate? Don't just hand a piece of writing to someone and say 'What do you think of this?' You'll get a more useful response if you make it clear that you'd expect some fault to be found, wouldn't be insulted by any criticism, and would do your best to make changes.

It's unlikely that there'll be anything seriously amiss, but do stress that you'd like a frank comment. You might get a response something like: 'Brilliant ... gripping ... fascinating ... but style rather pompous, can't work out William's relationship to George, a few words I can't understand', and so on. I hope that you'd rather take all this on board sooner rather than later; there may well be minor changes you could make at the outset that could save you a great deal of time, trouble and heartache later on. If you've spent months or years completing a mega-book on your family history and never shown any part of it to anyone, it may well be too late to make radical changes. Anyone you do show it to at that advanced stage may be overwhelmed by the bulk of it or may be less inclined to be honest about it because they know it's your much-loved baby – and you'd certainly be less inclined to re-write a vast amount of text.

You will be writing your book in cameos or sections over a period of time. You might not even compose the chapters in the final order in which they will appear, and your style or your sense of humour may change over weeks and months. At some point you'll have to weld all the pieces of your book together, creating a holistic product. Having edited each section to your satisfaction, you'll then have to sit down and read the whole thing through from start to finish. Are there inconsistencies? Have you repeated yourself? Has your writing style changed? Aim for a seamless robe.

◆ *Proof-reading*

What about proof-reading? The first time I ever wrote a book, I asked a friend who had once worked for a printing firm to proof-read the final manuscript. After all, he'd had experience, hadn't he? I know now why my friend only agreed to this request rather reluctantly. There is really no magic about proof-reading – it's just a laborious and time-consuming task.

Proof-read your own work, certainly, but also do everything you can to persuade friends and relations to carry out the same task for you, telling them that they needn't use any specialist hieroglyphics to indicate corrections, providing the meaning of their annotations is clear.

Different people spot different errors, and there's a lot to think about. Checking for factual accuracy (including, in particular, dates, addresses, web-site details and the like) is one thing; making sure that the text is clear is another. It really ought to be unambiguous, well-punctuated, free of grammatical howlers and with correct spelling.

Think about layout as well as content, and look out for 'typos' – that is, mechanical errors of typing – and double-check your page and footnote/endnote numbering.

If you feel confident enough, try to look for all these features at once – but be warned, it isn't easy. Your brain prefers to have its tasks separated, not all lumped together. If you're reading through looking for 'typos', don't for goodness' sake get too *interested* in what you're reading. That's fatal! You'll rush ahead to get to the next page, and your eye won't see, or your brain won't register, some glaring errors. There is even a rumour around that some professional proof-readers tackle a book from back to front, so that the sense doesn't get mixed up with the typographical accuracy!

Proof-reading, then, is not the same as simply reading. It requires a detached and objective approach; ideally the text should be read in a staccato way, each word being examined separately. Often it's the big errors that fail to get noticed, not the small ones. Ask anyone who proof-reads *Family Tree Magazine*, for example, as I do. If the team of proof-readers misses anything at all, it'll probably be some huge bold title, set in large-point type, not a small detail in the main text.

If you take your completed work to a commercial printer, he will expect you to read through his own 'proofs' before the presses start rolling. There should be few enough errors to spot at that stage – but try not to be lulled into a false sense of security as you carry out this final 'read', and do keep any 'author's corrections' to an absolute minimum.

◆ *A final thought*

Finally, here's something you'll just have to learn to live with: no matter how many times you read your text through, no matter how careful you are, no matter how many people do the job, the strong likelihood is that there will still be a few errors in the text on the day you publish. You'll probably spot these on the very next day – that's the unfairness of it all.

AN EXAMPLE OF FAMILY HISTORY WRITING

As we are now coming to the end of that part of this book which deals with the writing of a narrative, you might think it unfair of me if I were simply to offer you well-meant advice without giving you a brief example of my own work in this regard – so a short passage from my book *The Titford Family 1547-1947* (Phillimore, 1989) follows. This is not intended to be a classic example of good writing or anything of the kind; rather, I think you might find it interesting to consider the various sources I used in order to compile one single sentence.

Let me sketch the background very simply. In the year 1798 the worthy people of Frome in Somerset established a home-based fighting force called the Frome Selwood Volunteers, formed – in theory, at least – to help repulse an anticipated invasion by Napoleon and his troops. My namesake John Titford, second son of Charles Titford, cheesemonger and pig butcher, joined up as an infantryman. He may have been a brave volunteer, but he was not a healthy man, and on 2 February 1799 he died of consumption at the age of twenty-four and was buried with full military honours. My story continues like this:

> *It can have been no easy journey for the funeral procession of mourners and military volunteers as they followed the coffin up the steep climb to Catherine Hill Burial Ground that bleak Friday in February with the snow thick on the ground.* (p.98)

The question is this: where did the information contained in this sentence come from? Let's take a few words at a time:

'No easy journey'

The journey ended at the burial ground and would have started from the family home. Where was that? How do we know? At that time the Titfords lived at the first house on the east side of Pig Street, Frome, near the bridge. Notice that in days when a street worked for its living, its name was an uncompromising Pig Street, not Acacia Avenue or some such pretentious alternative. The detailed Frome rate books for the latter years of the 18th century establish this address for the family, information which is reinforced, as it happens, by a contemporary turnpike deed and by records of the Frome Literary Institute, which was eventually built on the site of the family house.

'Mourners and military volunteers'

How do we know that this was a military funeral? The family were practising Baptists throughout much of the 18th century, and are significantly absent from the baptismal and burial records of the parish church of St John – a bleak enough scenario for any family historian. However, the burial registers for Badcox Lane

Baptist Chapel in the town do exist for this period, and may be consulted at the Public Record Office in London and elsewhere. The Badcox Lane minister, John Kingdon, gave the kind of extra detail in his burial register that may not have appeared had this been recorded by the local Anglican clergyman:

John Titford. Aged 24. With Military Honours.

A list of volunteer infantrymen which appears in a printed history of the Frome Volunteers duly includes the name of 'John Tizford' (sic). Not only that, but across the road from the Titford home lay the Frome Bluecoat School, and the son of the master there, Edmund Crocker, kept a diary during this period, which has survived the ravages of time. His diary entry for 2 February reads:

On the 2d instant died in a consumption J Titford aged about 4 or 5 & 20 years. He being a volunteer in our infantry, he was this day interred with the military honours due to him.

'The steep climb to Catherine Hill Burial Ground'

How do we know that the climb was steep? Easy: visit the town, locate the old site of the burial ground and walk it for yourself!

'That bleak Friday'

How do we know that 2 February 1799 was a Friday? It's simply a matter of using a perpetual calendar of some sort; in this case I referred to that excellent publication, *Handbook of Dates for Students of English History* by C.R. Cheney (2000).

'With the snow thick on the ground'

How do we know there was snow? Local newspapers contain accounts of the appalling conditions prevailing at this time, with Frome suffering its heaviest fall of snow since 1767, and over in Norfolk, Parson Woodforde, the diarist, was writing that such severe weather had not been known for the last sixty years.

I hope you'll feel that this has been a useful example of how much information – information that may take weeks or months to unearth – can be compressed into just a few words. This is what I meant when I referred earlier to the act of synthesising your family history data into a narrative which is based upon fact but which will hopefully help the reader create a scene in his or her own mind. I've tried here to bring the past alive – or to bring it alive again, if you prefer.

I sometimes think that writing fiction would be easy; much of the time you'd be in control of the facts. Writing history or family history is different: the facts must be in control of you.

PREPARING TO PUBLISH YOUR FAMILY HISTORY

Now you've written your family story. Congratulations! This would be a good time to pause and take a breath before you carry on. Is there anything major that you've omitted? Are there any changes that you need to make now, before it's too late?

Whether or not you've asked friends or relations to read samples of your work as you've gone along, you might like to hand your completed script to someone you trust, asking for their honest opinion and for any suggestions for changes. Yes, I know you won't really want to alter anything so late in the day if you can possibly avoid it, but a calm and honest assessment at this stage could prove to be of great long-term benefit. If a friend doesn't point out a flaw or two now, a reviewer of your completed book may well do so later!

The task which now lies ahead is that of turning the family history you've written into a published book. Get ready, then, for a certain amount of extra concentrated effort, much of which is unavoidable whichever printing or publication option you decide to adopt.

To begin with, there will be some extra text to compile before you're through. I apologise for burdening you with such a thought, because by the time you've finished writing your main text, you're likely to be fairly tired, and also impatient to bring your project to some kind of conclusion.

The final stages of preparing a work for publication can be a frustrating time during which what we might call the 'near as dammit' syndrome sets in. Almost finished, but not quite ... Conversely, there might also be a slightly less obvious psychological dimension to it all: if you've worked on a book constantly for months or years, and you and your family have lived with it all that time, maybe deep down you don't really want to finish it? Back to an empty life. Oh dear ...

Be all that as it may, the job has to be done, and once you've finally, finally, finally finished it all, you should feel both relieved and elated, and can expect to be de-mob happy for weeks on end.

THE ELEMENTS OF A BOOK

What I'll do now is simply to move from the front of a book to the back, offering you a detailed list, complete with some explanatory comments, of what your finished book could contain. I say *could*, because not every publication will contain every single element mentioned here. Common sense should tell you that your book may not carry a dedication, but that it should have a title page – and so on.

◆ *A title*

You may have had a title in mind for your book right from the outset, or you may have finished all the writing and still be praying that inspiration will come. A title may come to you in a blinding flash, or you may need to sit down and consider the options very carefully. Why not ask a few friends and family members what they think? You can always turn down their suggestions politely if you need to.

When I wrote my book on the Titford family, I originally entitled it *Come Wind, Come Weather*, but when it was eventually published, it had become simply *The Titford Family 1547-1947*. I had some reservations about this at the time, but I knew that the publishers were keen that this book should sit alongside the many other publications they had on their lists with similar titles. In fact I think that neither title is ideal; *Come Wind, Come Weather* has a nice Bunyanesque ring to it, but tells you little enough about the content, while *The Titford Family* is rather bland, and suggests that the book covers all branches of the family, which it never intended to do.

I wish you many happy hours of thinking up a title. Here are a few invented examples, from the plain to the more ornate, to get you pondering:

> *The Fortescues; Fortescue Records; The Fortescue Family; The History of the Fortescue Family; The Fortescue Story; My Fortescues; The Fortescue Papers; The Fortescues of Essex; Fortescue and Related Families; Three Generations of Fortescues; Fortescues – London Goldsmiths; The Fighting Fortescues; Forte scutum salus ducum: the Fortescues of Devon; Born to Rule* (the name of Fortescue not mentioned); *A Devon Family* (the name of Fortescue not mentioned).

◆ *Front cover/dustjacket*

If you intend your book to be softback (that is, with covers made of paper, card, linen-effect card, laminated card or whatever), you will have a front cover to play with. Alternatively, you might be planning a hardback book with no dustjacket – or one with a dustjacket.

In each case, you'll have a front and back cover (softback or hardback) or a front and back of a dustjacket at your disposal. If a hardback book has a dustjacket, then the boards themselves (usually covered with cloth or simulated cloth) are very often plain.

Your title and the author's name will normally adorn the front cover/front of dustjacket, so that's a start. What else might you feature? A reproduction of a photograph, a drawing, a map? Do provide a caption for such an illustration on the dustjacket flap or at an appropriate place inside the book. For an impressive result you could superimpose the title and author's name on any illustration you use. On the other hand, you might decide to go for a very plain cover with minimal use of colour. If you do use a photograph, you could run it right to the very edges of the dustjacket or front board, a device known as 'bleeding off the edge'.

Producing an attractive and eye-catching cover could be an

expensive business if you want a full range of colours, but you might feel that it's worth the expense. They say you can't judge a book by its cover, but many a book has sold itself to a series of potential readers because it simply looks so nice as they pick it up.

The inside cover of a softback book is very often left blank, but it might contain a brief summary of the book's contents to give the reader a flavour of what is to come. The inside flap of a dustjacket is also very often used for this purpose.

Then there's the spine – if the book is thick enough to have one. This will feature the book title and the author's name; a dustjacket, if there is one, will repeat this information. If you've produced a fat and chunky book, you might be able to fit the words across the spine horizontally; if not, the reader will have to turn his head to one side to read the information as it runs up or down the spine. I say 'up or down', because there really is no consensus as to whether a title should read up the spine from the bottom, or down the spine from the top. In theory you might be able to fit the author's name across the top or bottom of the spine horizontally, leaving the title to run up or down beneath or above it. Anything that looks good is acceptable.

◆ *Preliminary pages ('prelims')*

Bibliographers refer to the first few pages of a book, those that come before the main text, as the 'prelims'. Pages which come between the title page and the main text (that is, the contents page, foreword, etc.) are sometimes un-numbered, but could begin at number 1, continuing uninterrupted thereafter once the main text begins. A more classical – classy, I would say – way of doing this is to number every page between the title and the main text with lower-case Roman numerals: i, ii, iii, iv, v, and so on. Look at one or two books, old and new, to see exactly what each one does in this regard.

◆ *Endpapers*

Open a case-bound (that is, hardback) book at the front. You'll notice that one piece of paper, twice the width of the book, has been folded vertically down the centre, one half being stuck to the front board, the other half standing free as the first 'page' of the book itself. These constitute the front 'endpapers'. The stuck-down half is referred to as the 'front pastedown', while the loose half is known as the 'front free endpaper'. It should come as no surprise to learn, therefore, that such a book will also have a rear pastedown and a rear free endpaper. Normally endpapers are left blank, but you could use them to feature an illustration or a map. A book with paper or card covers may well not have endpapers as such, though it will probably have a plain page bound in at the beginning and another at the end.

◆ Half-title page, or simply 'half title'

This is a sheet which simply carries the title of the book, and usually nothing else. A great favourite in times gone by, it is rather less commonly found now than it used to be.

◆ Title page

Here you'll find the title, in large print, and any sub-title in smaller print. There will also be the name of the author (or editor), and of any collaborators whose contribution to the finished work has been of significant value. The publisher will usually place his name (and his logo, if he has one) at the foot of the title page, often with the year of publication below it.

Over the years I have written many book reviews of privately-published family histories, and I must confess that I give those without a title page a hard time. Why spoil the ship for a ha'p'orth of tar? A book with no title page seems as incomplete as would a menu in a good quality restaurant that offered no starters, only the main course. Sometimes I come across family histories – and other published books and booklets on family history topics – which omit a title page and start the text on the first available left-hand page – even on the inside cover! It's easy to see why this should be so; in a way every page is vital, and we don't like leaving blank spaces. In my mind this is false economy.

Please, give your readers space in which to breathe! A good book, like a good meal, should be approached gently and steadily, gaining substance as it goes along.

If you were feeling really ambitious, you could even super-impose the words on your title page onto a faint background picture – an engraving or a drawing. Now we're getting very sophisticated!

◆ Reverse of the title page

This usually features a range of factual information of a bibliographical kind in which you should aim to provide:
- The name and address of the publisher.
- The date of publication of this and any earlier editions.
- Copyright symbol (a letter 'C' placed in a circle), together with the name of the person holding the copyright.
- An International Standard Book Number (ISBN).
- The name and address of the printer (as opposed to the publisher). This often comes below everything else at the foot of the rear-of-title page i.e. the title verso.

If you do decide to operate as your own publisher, you'll need to register your book for copyright purposes and obtain an International Standard Book Number, so let's go through the process now, while we're at this stage.

In most cases the copyright of a work is vested in the name of the author for life, and for a further seventy years after his or her death. For fuller information on copyright matters, see the latest edition of *Writers' and Artists' Yearbook*, which can be found in most public libraries.

As to establishing copyright as it relates to a specific publication, all UK and Irish publishers are obliged by law to send a copy of all new books (including serial titles) to the Legal Deposit Office, British Library, Boston Spa, Wetherby, West Yorkshire LS23 7BY (see the relevant web-site at www.bl.uk). In the course of time, the Copyright Libraries Agency, 100 Euston Street, London NW1 2HQ (www.ligc.org.uk/cla), acting on behalf of five other British Copyright Libraries (including the University Libraries of Oxford and Cambridge), will write to request that you send them further free copies under the terms of copyright legislation. You should comply willingly with this request. At least you will have the satisfaction of knowing that a copy of your book will be safely lodged in a number of libraries long after you've shuffled off this mortal coil and will duly appear on their catalogues, and also that it will be featured in the *British National Bibliography*, which is used by librarians and the book trade for stock selection.

It is not compulsory to obtain an International Standard Book Number (ISBN), but it's highly recommended, since it will act as a unique reference to distinguish your book from all others and will ensure that it is featured on bibliographic databases such as *Books in print*, which are used by libraries and the book trade to provide information to customers.

An ISBN always consists of ten digits, no more and no fewer, separated into four parts by spaces or by hyphens, and will normally appear on the rear of your title page and on the back cover of your book. When I wrote and published a series of books on Derbyshire dialect with a friend called Richard Scollins under the title of *Ey Up Mi Duck!* in the late 1970s, the first volume had the ISBN: 0 9505292 0 6. Here the first '0' identifies Britain, '9505292' is the number allocated to us as publishers, and '0 6' specifies the particular book.

In advance of the publication of your book (ideally, allow several weeks) write to ISBN Agency, Woolmead House West, Bear Lane, Farnham GU9 7LG (e-mail: isbn@whitaker.co.uk), requesting an application pack, which will include a form which should be completed and returned to the Agency by post (not by FAX or e-mail), together with a registration fee. If you are a new publisher, you will then be provided with your own publisher's ISBN prefix, supplemented by a further block of ISBN numbers, which you can use as unique identifiers for up to ten individual books. In the event, of course, you may only ever need to use one of these for the one-and-only book you publish, though you'll need a new ISBN for each *edition* (as opposed to each new *printing*) of an existing book, or if you decide to change the style of binding from hardback to softback or *vice versa*.

◆ *Dedication page*

A dedication, if there is one, will normally consist of just a few words, generously spaced, almost lost on an otherwise empty page. A dedication is no more essential to your book than is a key-note quotation (see below), but you may feel that it provides a unique opportunity for you to thank or to show great esteem for a particular person or group of people.

You may consider it appropriate to dedicate a book on family history to your parents or grandparents, your husband, wife, children or grandchildren. Whomever you decide upon, that person will probably be extremely grateful to you – even touched or moved by your gesture. You may want to add a short phrase after the person's name, something like: 'To Susan, who knows how much she has done to help make this book possible'. You may even make a dedication to your family at its broadest: 'To an exceeding great army of Champneys' or 'To all Carringtons far and wide'. Be guided by good taste and by the desire to make someone feel happy and even flattered.

◆ Reverse of the dedication page

This can either be left blank, or used for some appropriate purpose such as an appeal from the author to the readers to provide more information on the family in question if they possibly can. Alternatively, you could use the reverse of the dedication page for a 'key-note quotation'.

◆ Key-note quotation

I'm using this term to refer to a literary quotation of family history significance which you might use as the opening statement in your book. If you use one, preferably let it be one that means something to you, or is borne out by the book you have written.

My own family history book opened with that over-worked (though terribly appropriate) phrase used by Sherlock Holmes in Sir Arthur Conan Doyle's *The Sign of Four*:

When you have eliminated the impossible, whatever remains, however improbable, must be the truth.

Other old favourites include *Let us now praise famous men and our fathers that begat us* (Ecclesiasticus xliv, 1) or *No people will look forward to posterity who do not often look backward to their ancestors* (Edmund Burke), but perhaps you can find a rather less clichéd example to get you started? A search on the Internet using the words 'quotations family' would throw up examples such as: *Children rarely want to know who their parents were before they were parents, and when age finally stirs their curiosity, there is no parent left to tell them* (Russell Baker) or *Producing a child is not as hard as writing a book* (William Herbert Guthrie-Smith).

To make use of such a quotation to begin your book (or even at the start of each chapter?) isn't compulsory, but it's nice if you can find one that is particularly striking or which means something special to you.

◆ *Contents page*

List your sections and chapters, using one line for each, giving the page upon which each begins. If your book has not been arranged along logical lines, this should become immediately apparent from scanning your list of contents. Let's hope you don't have to confront this problem at such a late stage!

◆ *List of illustrations*

You may also wish to make a list of your illustrations, giving relevant page numbers. You could itemise your pedigrees separately if you wish.

◆ *Foreword*

A foreword, usually written by someone other than the author, is certainly not compulsory. Some dignitary or other may be prepared to endorse your book and sign his or her name at the bottom. The wording of the foreword may even be composed by you or by the publisher, requesting the busy dignitary simply to sign in agreement, yes or no!

◆ *Preface*

A preface could provide an opportunity for you to make some general statements about your book, your research, or your attitude towards the whole business. You could let it stand as an introduction to your book, or you could write an introduction in addition to, or instead of, a preface. Frequently a preface is followed by the name or initials of the author, together with a place and a date. This allows some authors to give the impression that they are forever lounging around writing books or prefaces in Bermuda or somewhere equally exotic, and that they are in the habit of referring to 4 August as 'St Nicodemus' Day' as a matter of course. If you insist on playing this game, do avoid Pancake Day or April Fools' Day as the date for a preface, won't you?

◆ *Acknowledgements*

Do be careful here. Either mention almost no one, or mention absolutely everyone. It's rather like sending out invitations to a wedding; most people will accept it if you explain that you plan to have a very small family wedding; what they won't happily accept is a situation in which friends of yours, whom they consider to be no closer in friendship to you than they are, receive an invitation if they don't. So if you go for comprehensive and detailed acknowledgements, do try to miss no one out.

The only safe thing to do is to collect the names of those you will acknowledge as you go along; eventually you can go back over your old correspondence and pluck out any names you might have overlooked. You'll probably end up thanking certain people even though their contributions have been fairly minimal – just because you think it would be a nice thing or the right thing to do, and would give the named person real pleasure. The whole thing is a minefield, so do take it seriously. Acknowledgements relating to certain illustrations you have used can be incorporated in your main list, or given separately.

◆ *List of subscribers*

If you've launched your book by way of collecting advanced subscriptions, then a cheap and effective way of thanking subscribers for their confidence in you is to print a list of their names. This is a time-honoured practice, and the subscribers' lists of books published in previous centuries can make fascinating reading.

In what order do you place the names? An alphabetical list would seem to be an eminently sensible device, but sometimes names appear in the order in which their subscriptions were received. If your subscription copies are numbered, then you would usually put the appropriate number against each person's name. Books published in a 'limited edition' are often highly prized by collectors; just remember, however, that a short print-run limited edition may simply indicate that the author or publisher, rather strapped for cash, is making a virtue out of a necessity!

You may, if you wish, choose to feature acknowledgements and a list of subscribers at the back of your book, rather than at the front.

◆ *Introduction*

Your introduction will be written last of all. Yes, really! You cannot possibly know what you're introducing until you've written it. If you sit down to write a family history and struggle over the introduction at the outset, you'll probably get frustrated and disheartened. Leave it until the end.

You may have had some general thoughts about family history or about the writing of a family history as work has progressed; in the introduction, try sharing these thoughts with your readers.

The deeper I became mentally and even emotionally involved in the process of writing my own family history, the stronger grew the odd but not unpleasant feeling that my ancestors almost seemed to be at my elbow as I wrote about them. Thus it was that I used the word 'eerie' in the opening paragraph of my introduction:

The canonization of Oedipus as the patron saint of family historians is long overdue; his quest for self-knowledge through an unravelling of the mysteries of his origins is essentially the same as that undertaken in a more modest way and with less harrowing consequences by thousands of 20th-century family researchers. Genealogy is, of course, a subject of enormous fascination whichever family we might be investigating; yet there can be something especially moving and almost eerie about tracing our own direct ancestry, warts and all.

In 1995 my cousin Donald Titford of Bath published *Moonrakers in My Family*, his account of various branches of the Titford family not covered in detail in my own book. Donald is as prone to a touch of philosophical pondering as I am, and his introduction opens like this:

Most stories start at the beginning and finish at the end. A family history is different. It starts in the middle and ends when the author decides to cry 'finis'. Its true beginning is lost in the mists of time and the end has yet to come.

Your introduction will no doubt be different again, born of your own reflections as you think back upon what will probably have been a long and even exhausting process of writing the story of your ancestors.

Why not use part of your introduction to deal with topics which wouldn't seem to fit naturally anywhere else? Might this be the place to examine the geographical occurrence of the family name at different periods in time, or to present some ideas as to the origins and meaning of the surname?

◆ *The main text*

At last your 'main text' appears, complete with footnotes/endnotes, as appropriate. This will be the story you have to tell; it will constitute the bulk of the book, and is essentially what the whole thing is all about.

Give careful thought to your chapter or section headings. Do they encapsulate the information which follows? Will you print them in large bold type? Are they phrased in a consistent way? There's no point in having one chapter entitled *Thomas of Norwich*, while the next one is worded differently, reading something like: *The Story of William of Swaffham (1765-1842)*.

Will you use subheadings within chapters? Will you print them in bold type or italics? Try not to use only one subheading in the first chapter, but twelve in the second. Aim for balance.

Will you indent longer quotations within the text? Will you print them in italics? Whichever decision you make, stick to it and be consistent. It may look as if a finished book which you buy in a shop is professionally arranged and presented as if by magic, but its professionalism will be the result of a great deal of careful attention to detail.

Number your pages. Anyone who wishes to quote from your book, or to refer to it for specific information – or to use your index – will need to have a page number reference. Make life easy for others! Each number may be placed centrally at the top or bottom of a page, or – very commonly – at the top right hand corner of each right-hand page and at the top left-hand corner of each left-hand page.

Let page one be on the right-hand side. It's a time-honoured practice that the first page of the main body of your text should start on a right-hand page, and be numbered as page one. Thereafter all right-hand pages will carry odd numbers, while all left-hand pages will carry even numbers.

◆ *Illustrations*

If you possibly can, you ought to consider embellishing your text with a variety of illustrations, the reproduction of which should prove no great difficulty either to a publisher, or to you if you publish your book yourself. The use of computer scanners and digital cameras is now commonplace; if you have the requisite expertise you could make use of such technology yourself, or else employ a professional to integrate text and illustrations for you by way of desk-top publishing software.

Illustrations can usually be made to occupy as much or as little space on a page as you wish – providing that any printed or manuscript words they contain remain legible. Some illustrations merit a whole page to themselves; others don't. It's certainly not ideal to bunch all your pictures together in just a few pages – this was the method commonly adopted by publishers in the days when they had to use glossy art paper to ensure maximum quality of reproduction. Ideally your illustrations should punctuate your text, and be placed as close as possible to the reference which is made to them in the story. Do give each illustration a caption which explains what it is, and maybe its significance, too. Tell the reader what he or she is looking at. Place your caption underneath the illustration, if possible; if not, put it above or to

Can you find an illustration of a church or chapel where your ancestors worshipped? (Cross Street (Unitarian) Chapel, Manchester, in 1856. From Memorials of a Dissenting Chapel *by Sir Thomas Baker. 1884.)*

one side, or even on the opposite or neighbouring pages if you have to, but always make it clear (using small arrows if you like) exactly which caption refers to which illustration.

You might consider using any or all of the following kinds of illustrations:

• *Facsimiles of manuscript documents*

These can add a great deal of atmosphere to any family history, especially if they are visually striking as well as historically interesting. Why not use your book to act as a showcase for documents which you have in your own private possession but which have never previously seen the light of day? If you do wish to use facsimiles of documents held by various public repositories, you'll need written permission and may have to pay a reproduction fee. In any case, you should refer to the original holder of such documents in your acknowledgements.

Facsimile illustration, reproduced
with permission and with a frame

Portrait format,
long edge running
vertically

Generous margins, top,
bottom and sides

Running title (or head)

MOONRAKERS IN MY FAMILY

MANOR COURT OF WYLE. 18TH JUNE 1764
William Titford, Shepherd to the East End Field, is presented
(WRO 2057/M54)

his identity into the open but it had also persuaded the Court to emphasise that the Custom of the
Manor applied to William Titford specifically – just in case he should consider that a free breakfast
on Sunday and the skins of any dead sheep placed him beyond the Court's jurisdiction. The
'presentment' reads:

'They present William Titford, Shepherd to the East end fflock, for ffeeding his fflock of sheep on the Cowdown
contrary to the Custom of this Manor, he having been presented for the like default att two last General Courts held
for this Manor, and that he hath incurred the penalty of 5/–d. for so doing, and they now order the said Shepherd
shall not feed the said Cowdown with his said fflock contrary to the said Custom under further penalty of 5/–d. for
each default.'[13]

The Manor Court of Wylye was wasting its time. Once again William the Pauper completely
disregarded the Court's judgement and continued in his wicked ways. The Earl of Pembroke's
steward persevered, however, and the following year, at the meeting of the Manor Court held on
24th June 1765 – the anniversary of the baptism of William's dead son, James – William the Pauper
was again presented. This time they spelt his name wrong!

Also they present that William Tidford, Shepherd of the East end fflock of sheep, was presented and amersed at the
last General Court held in this Manor for ffeeding his said fflock of sheep on the Cowdown contrary to the Custom of
the said Manor, and because he has again been guilty of the like offence, they do therefore further amerse him five
shillings.'[14]

By the time of the next meeting of the General Court of the Manor on 19th May 1766 the Clerk
must have been praying for the rubber stamp to be invented. Already he had lost count of the
number of times William the Pauper had been presented, but it didn't really matter since the
Shepherd of the East end fflock continued to disregard the verdict of the Court and his annual
presentment had now become a mere matter of routine. Nevertheless, at their meeting on 9th May
1766, the Manor Court conscientiously went through the motions of presenting William the Pauper
as usual:

Title for illustration and a brief
description of contents. Wilts.
Record office document reference number

Number referring to notes
at the end of the book

Quotation, indented
and in small type

Main text in a classic serif
typeface, not too large or small.
Lines spaced neither too close
nor too far apart

A typical page from a published family history. (Moonrakers in My Family by
D.G. Titford, 1995.)

- *Facsimiles of printed documents or books*

You might like to use newspaper obituaries, extracts from commercial directories, printed broadsides, posters, theatre programmes, Masonic lodge cards, 'loving memory' cards, poll books and the rest.

- *Photographs*

You might use photographs of your ancestors (or of yourself and your own family), singly or in groups. What better way to bring your family history alive than to arrange for great-grandmother to be staring out of the page at us, be she ever so stern and on her dignity, or sporting a dimply smile as a result of the photographer's urgings.

Photographs of people doing things are often more intriguing than mere studio portraits – there's great uncle Fred failing to catch a beach ball thrown by his nephew Billie! If you feature a group photograph, do your best to name as many people in it as you can, and also consider using local views such as photographs of schools, churches, cars, bicycles, charabancs, or local events such as carnivals, Temperance Society marches, Sunday School outings or war victory celebrations – even if your own ancestors don't actually appear in them.

For help in dating old photographs, you should refer to *Family History in Focus* by Don Steel and Lawrence Taylor (1984), *Dating Old Photographs* by Robert Pols (2nd edition, 1998) and *Fashion à la Carte 1860-1900* (catch the pun in the title?) by Avril Lansdell (1985). I'd also recommend the regular 'Practical picture dating' feature by Jean Debney which appears each month in *Practical Family History* magazine.

If you do possess old portrait photographs, you will regard them as special and valued treasures. It would make sense to have the most precious ones copied – especially if you plan to hand one over to a printer or publisher for inclusion in your book. Faded photographs can often be given new life and greater contrast in this way. You may decide to take some photographs yourself, especially if some of the old family homes or haunts are still extant, or if the local churchyard is bristling with gravestones which commemorate your ancestors.

• *Paintings, engravings, etchings, sketches and drawings*

You may have some nice paintings or drawings of family relevance tucked away somewhere? You may not have a portrait in oils, and no one may have bequeathed you a charming portrait of great grandmother on a miniature, but can you find a sketch of Auntie Ada, or one drawn *by* Auntie Ada? Maybe there is an autograph album somewhere with such treasures in it? Do you have drawings or paintings of the family home or its immediate neighbourhood? Sketches of family pets? Family cars?

Or perhaps you have the skills to enhance the text with a few pictures of your own? Drawings of a church or a house? Even a conjectural picture of what you believe your great-great grandfather might have looked like (based, perhaps, on photographs of his sons which are in your possession)? Some authors like to include a cartoon or two in order to add a touch of light relief to their book. That's up to you.

Do remember that not all facsimiles or other illustrations you use need name or feature anyone in your family specifically. They could simply add a flavour of the environment in which your ancestors moved. They could suggest that great grandfather would have signed an apprenticeship indenture like this, worked at a trade like this, worn a jacket like this, lived in a street like this, gone to a school like this, travelled in a tram like this, shopped at a shop like this, fought on a battlefield like this.

• *Maps*

There's nothing quite like a good detailed map for bringing alive the area in which your ancestors lived and moved and had their being. Try and obtain one for the appropriate period or periods if you can, and identify the places where various family members were settled if you can find this out. If not, why not attempt to draw a simple uncluttered map of your own?

It might also suit your purposes to include a map covering a wider area – a county or a region, for example. This will give a broader context, and you may want to reproduce a regional or a national map on which you have marked family migration patterns or major concentrations of a particular surname at certain periods.

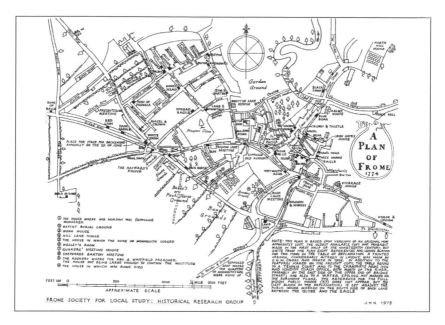

Detailed local maps can really bring an area alive. This reconstructed map of Frome, Somerset, as it was in 1774, was published in 1978.

- **Pedigrees**

For the purpose of illustrating your book, it would seem ideal to make use of pedigrees of some kind, in whatever format suits you best. These can be of enormous value to the reader, who needs to have a clear picture of family relationships. Ideally you would draw one overall simplified pedigree covering the entire family story, then a series of more detailed ones featuring two or three generations at a time. Space these out throughout the text if you can; if not, group them together at the end.

- **Heraldry**

If armorial bearings have been associated with your family, it would be a crying shame not to feature these somewhere in your book. Have you inherited some silver or china bearing a crest, a bookplate, or a seal matrix ring? Be careful, though: coats of arms were not granted to families as such – they were awarded to

Is there evidence of heraldry having been used in your family? This signet ring owned by Mike Buckler of Waimaiku, New Zealand, features a family crest originally granted to his forebear Sir Walter Buckler of Causeway, Dorset, in 1544.

individuals for their own use, and descend thereafter to all male offspring in succeeding generations. In Scotland, such descent only passes through the eldest son in each generation; younger sons have to 'matriculate' the arms of the head of their house with a suitable heraldic 'difference', which is assigned according to specific rules. So there is no such thing as a Bloggs family coat of arms.

You may well want to spare yourself the expense of reproducing a coat of arms in full colour, in which case help is at hand. If you wish, you can 'trick' the arms, which involves the use of abbreviations to indicate the colours, metals and furs, or you can use what is known as the 'Petra Sancta' method, which uses lines, dots and other hatching for the same purpose.

If you don't want to be accused of going over the top, I would caution against letting a full-colour armorial adorn the front cover or front dustjacket of your book unless the arms are yours by inheritance or have been granted to you personally.

◆ Conclusion

A good conclusion, appearing at the end of your main text, will draw all the threads together; it may summarise the family story in a few sentences, or it may define a few themes that have been running through the book. It will take some careful thought before you write a conclusion, but it will be well worth the effort. Call it 'Conclusion' or 'Final thoughts' – or whatever seems appropriate.

◆ Addenda

You may well not need to make use of addenda, but if you have discovered some information which is vital to your story at a stage when it is simply too late to change your text, you could off-load this vital material in an addendum or two. The alternatives would be not to mention it at all, or perhaps to rewrite large sections of text. Remember: you won't stop discovering vital information just because you've written a book!

◆ Endnotes

If you've decided to make use of endnotes rather than footnotes, these can appear after any addenda and before any appendices.

◆ Appendices

I won't say that appendices are a dumping ground, exactly, but they do provide an excellent opportunity for you to include material in your book without its having to clog up the main text and interrupt the flow. In this sense, they're rather like expanded footnotes or endnotes.

A sketch or photograph of a memorial inscription can make an interesting illustration. (From Memorials of the old meeting house and burial ground, Birmingham *by Catherine Hutton Beale. 1882.)*

During your research you may have transcribed a number of wills and/or probate inventories, for example. You probably won't want to include these in full in your main text, so you can relegate them to an appendix. You may have other lists or transcripts that can be dealt with in the same way. Number your appendices and, unless they're very short, use a new page to begin each one if you can. Where necessary give some indication in the main text that an appendix contains expanded or extra information.

◆ *Bibliography*

You may have read, or dipped into, several books which you've found to be relevant to your story, or you may have consulted only a few. Either way, it's a good idea to list them in a bibliography, however brief. This will show that you've done some reading around the subject, and will point your keener readers to sources they might like to consult for themselves. The usual conventions for a bibliography are:

– List the books by surname of author, alphabetically.

– Put the author's surname first, then his or her first name or initials, then the title of the book or other published work (in italics if you can arrange this; underlined if you have no other choice), then the edition, if relevant, then the year of publication (put 'n.d.' for 'no date' if this is not specified). You can add the name of the publisher before the year of publication if you wish, though increasingly I tend not to do this myself.

Here is an example of a typical entry presented in this way:

Steinberg, S.H. *Historical tables, 58 BC – AD 1961.* 6th ed. (1961).

This kind of bibliographical arrangement is one which you will commonly find adopted in scholarly works, though alternative models have gained some popularity in recent years.

How many words in a book-title should begin with a capital letter? Well, obviously, the first word of the title, place names and personal names. The main thing, however, is to be

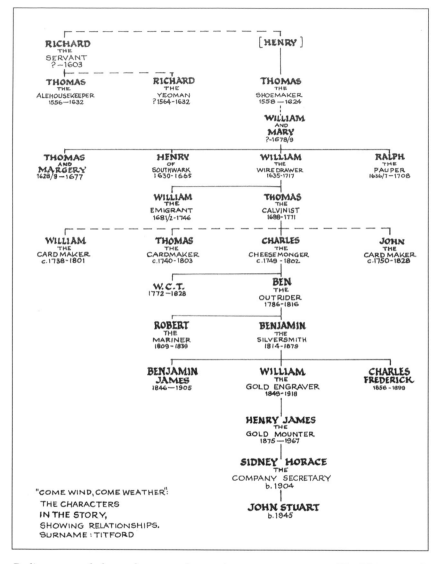

RICHARD
THE
SERVANT
? −1603

[HENRY]

THOMAS
THE
ALEHOUSEKEEPER
1556−1632

RICHARD
THE
YEOMAN
?1564-1632

THOMAS
THE
SHOEMAKER
1558 −1624

WILLIAM
AND
MARY
?-1678/9

THOMAS
AND
MARGERY
1628/9−1677

HENRY
OF
SOUTHWARK
1630-1665

WILLIAM
THE
WIRE DRAWER
1635-1717

RALPH
THE
PAUPER
1636/7−1708

WILLIAM
THE
EMIGRANT
1681/2-1746

THOMAS
THE
CALVINIST
1688-1771

WILLIAM
THE
CARD MAKER
c.1738-1801

THOMAS
THE
CARDMAKER
c.1740-1803

CHARLES
THE
CHEESE MONGER
c.1749-1802

JOHN
THE
CARD MAKER
c.1750-1828

W.C.T.
1772−1828

BEN
THE
OUTRIDER
1786-1816

ROBERT
THE
MARINER
1809−1839

BENJAMIN
THE
SILVERSMITH
1814-1879

BENJAMIN
JAMES
1846−1905

WILLIAM
THE
GOLD ENGRAVER
1849-1918

CHARLES
FREDERICK
1856-1899

HENRY JAMES
THE
GOLD MOUNTER
1875−1967

SIDNEY HORACE
THE
COMPANY SECRETARY
b. 1904

JOHN STUART
b.1945

"COME WIND, COME WEATHER":
THE CHARACTERS
IN THE STORY,
SHOWING RELATIONSHIPS.
SURNAME : TITFORD

Pedigrees can help readers to understand your story more readily. This example from The Titford family 1547-1947 *(1989) features all the male Titfords around whom the story* (Come Wind, Come Weather) *is based, each of whom has a chapter named after him: 'Richard the Servant', 'Thomas the Alehousekeeper', and so on.*

consistent throughout. To adopt any other way of doing things is almost bound to lead to inconsistencies. So you'll see that in the Steinberg example quoted above, I have only used a capital letter to begin the word 'Historical', leaving 'tables' without a capital.

By all means classify the bibliography if it contains a large number of titles (for example: London; Hertfordshire; Kent; General), and treat pamphlets in much the same way as books.

Try not to use a bibliography to show off your erudition and the breadth of your reading! If a book has been useful and relevant, include it; if it hasn't, exclude it.

◆ *Glossary*

I made reference earlier in this book to the fact that a certain number of your readers may find the world of family history a strange one, full of words or references which are unfamiliar. One way of making life easier for such people is to provide a brief glossary – make it an appendix if you like. Spell out what an 'admon' is, explain the Hearth Tax, Hardwicke's Marriage Act, a removal order and a bastardy bond; say when the 19th century censuses were taken, unravel the mysteries of the IGI. This should help your inexperienced readers make sense of what you're saying, and you may well feel that it's preferable to use a glossary for this purpose rather than explaining unfamiliar terms in the main text as you go along.

◆ *Index*

We must work on the assumption that an index to your book is highly desirable. Some book reviewers will slate any publication that doesn't have one. That seems rather unfair, given the time and effort necessary to compile such an index, but family historians should be very well aware that the usefulness of a book to other researchers is increased a hundredfold if it carries an index.

So do make every effort to compile an index. Do the work yourself if you like, either manually or by using a computer programme, or else pay a professional to do it for you. That could be money well spent. Either way, you can't compile an index until

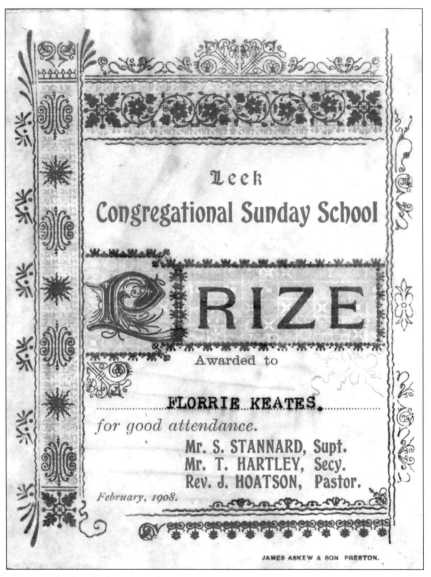

A copy of a bookplate pasted into a School or Sunday School prize awarded to a member of your family could make an attractive illustration. Florrie Keates of Leek Congregational Sunday School in Staffordshire was given just such a prize 'for good attendance' in February 1908.

the book is in an advanced stage of completion; you must be sure that the pagination of the book (you will number the pages, won't you?) is finalised before creating an index that refers the reader to specific pages.

◆ *The back end*

At the end of your book, the 'back end' as I might unofficially call it, you will have some space to fill if you wish to fill it. Do remember, however, that using every available blank space in a book can make it look cluttered and can so easily detract from any classical dignity it might otherwise have achieved.

The spaces theoretically available to you are:

On a softback book or a hardback book with no dustjacket: the inside rear cover and the back cover.

On a hardback book with a dustjacket: the rear inside flap of the dustjacket and the rear cover of the dustjacket.

You could use all or some – or none – of this space productively if you so wish. You might decide to include some of the following elements, but do try to be guided by the 'minimal clutter' principle:

• A brief summary of what the book is all about. This could certainly be of use to potential readers, and if you add a few commendatory remarks about your own work, singing its praises and saying what a vital contribution it makes to the fund of human knowledge, you'll have thus produced a 'blurb', as they call it in the publishing trade.

• A biography of the author. This needn't be long and needn't be deadly serious. Include a photograph if you like. Such biographies are frequently seen on the inside rear flaps of dustjackets.

• Source of supply. It's certainly prudent to inform readers where copies of the book in question may be obtained, if not from the publisher (whose address would normally appear on the back of the title page). Perhaps some kind person has offered to take a stock of the books and post them out to customers? Give a name and address, and also a telephone/fax number and/or an e-mail address if you wish.

• Advertisements. This may be your one and only book, but if you've published others, then don't miss a golden opportunity to advertise them for sale. Indeed, you could use some of the space available to you to advertise almost anything. You might be happy enough to accept some financial help from a retail business or an organisation in exchange for advertising space (used tastefully). If not you might, for example, care to advertise your paid services as a genealogist or record agent, or as a searcher in indexes you have created.

• The price of your book. This should be indicated somewhere, normally on the back cover (or on the inside front flap of a dustjacket). Not all publishers these days choose to print a price in this way, but if inflation does take a sharp upward turn and you still have stocks of your book left unsold, you can always use stickers showing a higher price if you feel you must.

You may not wish to fill the back cover/back of dustjacket with text, but would rather leave it blank. Alternatively, you might wish to use it for an extra illustration, or you might choose to carry over a front-cover illustration in a 'wrap round' fashion. This can be most effective, and is not uncommon.

So much, then, for what I hope has been a comprehensive list of all the elements that could make up a book. Remember again that it's a matter of 'could', not 'must', and that you also have at least some discretion regarding the exact order in which you place the components that I've listed.

FINANCE

You have now reached a very significant staging-post on your journey; you've written a family history and you've assembled all the extra components that will help transform it into a book, though you don't yet have what we might call a completed 'product' as such. What lies ahead is a related but separate process – that of publication.

Let's try to define what 'publishing' means. It's the process whereby a book is printed and bound, advertised, marketed, distributed and sold. You'll need to decide at some point how

If you have the skill, why not use drawings of your own to illustrate your book?
(From Moonrakers in My Family *by D.G. Titford. 1995.)*

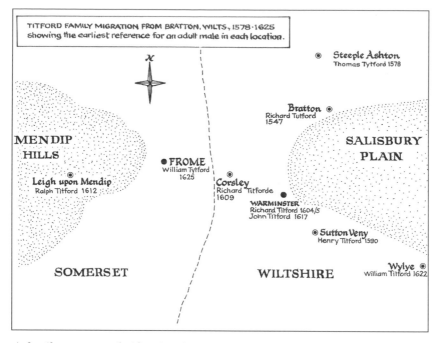

A family map can clarify migration patterns and give readers some idea of the geography involved. (From The Titford Family 1547-1947 *(1989).)*

much of this process you feel able to undertake yourself, but beyond the question of how much effort, time and skill you can devote to it all lies the crucial consideration as to how much finance you can raise to get things off the ground. We'd better think about this right at the start.

It's clear that carrying out every stage of the book production yourself will be the cheapest option, whereas using a publisher will be the most expensive, unless – and this is unlikely for the history of an individual family – he will invest some of his own capital in the venture. Publishing is no different from any other human enterprise: if you want high quality, and if you want someone else to spend his time and apply his expertise, it will cost you.

How will you finance your book? Consider the following options:

◆ Self-financing

Pay for it entirely yourself, with or without a loan of some kind.

◆ Help from the family

Persuade other family members to share the financial burden with you. This could be distant cousins at home or abroad who have a particular interest or who are as keen to see the family history in print as you are. You may have a parent or an uncle or aunt who would be persuaded by an argument that ran: 'Look, you've always said that you'd leave me a bit of a legacy in your will; wouldn't it be a good idea if you were to make a small donation now towards the publishing of this book? That would bring pleasure to you, to me, to the kids and to other members of the family.' You'll know better than I whether such arguments – which seem to me to be very reasonable – would cut any ice with your nearest and dearest. Certainly some parents feel they would rather see the smile on the face of their children or grandchildren in this life than have to imagine such a smile from the depths of the grave.

◆ Sponsorship

Find a wealthy sponsor. Shakespeare and many another great author did it, so why not you? You may have contacted that fabled rich cousin living in America, or had some correspondence with a distant relative who made a fortune from his biscuit factory. Could they help out? Would a well-known company bearing your distinctive family name and with some distant relationship feel inclined to help you publish a quality book which they might even use as a promotional aid?

◆ Local funding

If your family history features one particular locality very strongly, perhaps some individual or organisation in that place will help out in some way?

◆ Subscription

You could offer the book to subscribers in advance of publication, thereby adopting a potentially viable strategy with a long history behind it.

Once your book is written, and before you've spent too much money on its production, prepare an advertising flier or leaflet which extols the virtues of your product. State how the book will

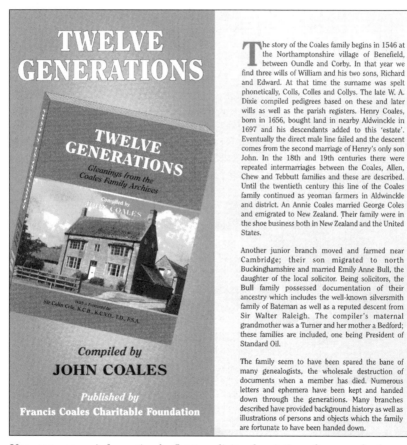

TWELVE GENERATIONS

Gleanings from the Coales Family Archives

Compiled by
JOHN COALES

Published by
Francis Coales Charitable Foundation

The story of the Coales family begins in 1546 at the Northamptonshire village of Benefield, between Oundle and Corby. In that year we find three wills of William and his two sons, Richard and Edward. At that time the surname was spelt phonetically, Colls, Colles and Collys. The late W. A. Dixie compiled pedigrees based on these and later wills as well as the parish registers. Henry Coales, born in 1656, bought land in nearby Aldwinckle in 1697 and his descendants added to this 'estate'. Eventually the direct male line failed and the descent comes from the second marriage of Henry's only son John. In the 18th and 19th centuries there were repeated intermarriages between the Coales, Allen, Chew and Tebbutt families and these are described. Until the twentieth century this line of the Coales family continued as yeoman farmers in Aldwinckle and district. An Annie Coales married George Coles and emigrated to New Zealand. Their family were in the shoe business both in New Zealand and the United States.

Another junior branch moved and farmed near Cambridge; their son migrated to north Buckinghamshire and married Emily Anne Bull, the daughter of the local solicitor. Being solicitors, the Bull family possessed documentation of their ancestry which includes the well-known silversmith family of Bateman as well as a reputed descent from Sir Walter Raleigh. The compiler's maternal grandmother was a Turner and her mother a Bedford; these families are included, one being President of Standard Oil.

The family seem to have been spared the bane of many genealogists, the wholesale destruction of documents when a member has died. Numerous letters and ephemera have been kept and handed down through the generations. Many branches described have provided background history as well as illustrations of persons and objects which the family are fortunate to have been handed down.

You can use an informative leaflet to solicit subscriptions for your forthcoming publication. This advertising flier (originally printed in full colour) was distributed by John Coales in 2000, and his splendid family history book was duly published soon afterwards.

be bound (you could offer softback and hardback alternatives at different prices), approximately how many pages it will have, what kind of illustrations it will contain. Invite anyone who reads your leaflet to subscribe at a reduced pre-publication price which they should send in advance direct to you or to someone who may do the job for you. Quote an overall price including postage and packing, not forgetting that good quality padded mail bags are not cheap!

Anyone interested should give their details on a tear-off slip and send the money without delay. You must specify the pre-publication price, then, but needn't be exact about any final published price – 'Approximately £20' would suffice. There's no point in tying your hands at this stage. Give an expected publication date and also a closing date for your offer which is not too close in time, but not too far away, in case people leave your leaflet lying around and then forget about it. Say that the names of subscribers will be printed in the book if and when it is published, and ask the subscriber to specify how he or she would like this entry to read. You can number subscribers' copies if you wish – that does make them feel rather special and exclusive. Some generous souls may want to pay for more than one copy, and may provide you with the names of various members of their family accordingly.

You'll probably wish to say that you consider this book to be an important contribution to the history of the family, but that publication in this form will be an expensive undertaking, and will be dependent upon a sufficient number of subscribers coming forward.

All this presupposes that you've decided which form of publication you'd like to go for if it could be afforded, and that you've costed the whole thing accordingly. If you're going to take the trouble to solicit subscriptions, you'll probably have opted to use a publisher, or a printer at least. If the subscription strategy fails, you can fall back on cheaper methods of production.

Post copies of such a flier to any relations or friends you can think of; if your surname is unusual, consider sending a copy to everyone of that surname you can find in telephone directories across the country, and even abroad. If your book has featured one town or village very prominently, send a copy or copies to the local newspaper in case they can make a story out of it or feature it in some way. You could produce a professionally-printed single-sheet flier and pay to have one inserted in family history magazines or journals. That will cost money, of course, and you might decide that it would be too large a financial gamble to take for your modest family history.

If the response to your pre-publication offer is healthy, you can go ahead and publish in whatever way you have decided, posting subscribers their copies as soon as you can. If the response is borderline, you may have some hard thinking to do. If very few people express an interest, you may simply have to reimburse the few faithful supporters and think again. It could well be that it's only once your subscribers have responded that you'll know whether you can afford to produce your book using one of the more expensive options open to you.

PUBLISHING OPTIONS

Once you have made a realistic assessment of the financial commitment you are prepared to make, you'll have a better idea of what publishing options are viable. Essentially you have two choices, as follows:

◆ Using a publisher

Let's get the question of a publisher dealt with straightaway. Do you really need one, and if you do, will he take the financial strain, or will he expect you to take all or some of it? Make no mistake, few if any printed family histories are going to make much of a profit for anyone, and publishers are in business to make money, not to dispense philanthropy. You could send a synopsis of your book to an established publisher, but you might well receive a rejection slip in return, or a request for a large sum of money to carry out what in effect could be a form of 'vanity publishing'. You may receive unsolicited mail from a vanity publisher; some have the bare-faced cheek to ask you to pay thousands of pounds up front, but then proudly inform you that you'll get a generous 'royalty' on all copies sold. Take a look at

Did a portrait of an ancestor ever appear in a magazine or journal? Gustavus Armstrong, born in Enniskillen, Fermanagh, Ireland, became a Methodist minister in 1792 and died on 25 March 1832. He is featured here in the Methodist Magazine *at the age of 28.*

offers like this if you like, but make sure there's a waste-paper bin or an open fire handy as you do so.

There is nothing quite so satisfying as seeing your book appear over the imprint of a well-known publisher (I was delighted with Phillimore's professional approach to the publication of my work on the Titford family), but many books would never have seen the light of day if their authors hadn't taken the bull by the horns and published their own work themselves. A publisher will certainly take some of the strain, will knock your book into shape and should have the wherewithal to handle advertising, selling and distribution effectively, but even if you can convince him that your book is a good bet, he will also take a fair amount of the money, too. That's no cause for complaint – it's just part of the reality of the market place.

If you do use a publisher, he should make a distinction between that which he needs you to provide, and that which he will do for you. Ask him exactly what he wants from you; he'll probably be delighted to have your text on a compatible computer disk, and may tell you how you should present the illustrations and other bits and pieces that make up the final book.

◆ *Self-publishing*

You could decide to publish the book yourself, which will mean that you will take responsibility for each stage of the process. That doesn't necessarily mean that you'll have to do all the work yourself, of course, any more than a commercial publisher would. You could be bold enough to produce the book entirely under your own steam, duplicating and binding copies in a form that you find acceptable. Alternatively, you could take your completed book to any printer you can find who will offer you reasonable terms for a short print-run. Unless you hand him a computer disk and let him do the 'typesetting' for you, you'll have to produce camera-ready copy – that is, text and illustrations which can be duplicated or photographed exactly as they stand to create plates for the off-set printing machine. A cheaper option would be to take the same camera-ready copy (or a computer disk) to a reprographics shop which has the facility to produce copies by means of photocopying, and may also bind separate sheets into a book for you.

PRODUCING A MASTER COPY

We're moving along. You now have all the elements necessary to produce a book, and the time is approaching when you'll have to make some final decisions. Will you use a commercial publisher, or handle it all yourself? And whichever of these options you choose, might you now feel inclined to dump everything you've produced in a box, and simply hand it all over to your publisher or printer to do with as he will? That would be a shame, don't you think? You would lose control of the process and would be incurring extra costs. I'll assume, instead, that you may have just enough energy left to consider taking the process one stage further yourself by producing a 'camera-ready' master copy of your work which can then be used without much alteration by a publisher, printer or reprographic shop.

◆ *Decisions . . .*

If you are brave enough to take the 'master copy' route, there'll be a few aspects of the process to think about and some decisions to make, as usual. Here they are:

• *Format*

I'm using the word here to refer to 'landscape' format, in which the book has its shorter edge running vertically, and its longer edge horizontally, or 'portrait', where the long edge runs vertically and the short edge runs horizontally. In other words, a landscape book has a short spine and wide floppy pages, whereas a portrait book has a long spine and feels tall. Of the two, portrait is by far the commonest. It feels right somehow. Landscape can work well for illustrations that have more width than height, and could be ideal for pedigrees. That being said, I'd strongly advise that you stick with the old familiar portrait format.

This might be the place to mention the fact that you could arrange your text into columns; indeed, you'll almost certainly have to if you use a landscape format. Reading a long line of text can be tiring and dispiriting. Most word processor and desk top publishing packages will offer you the facility of creating columns.

• *Page size*

There seems to be little enough uniformity these days with regard to page size – just look at the books in your public library. It will probably suit you, for all that, to work with one of the standard metric paper sizes established several years ago by the British Standards Institution and with which British (but not American) readers will now be very familiar.

A metric sheet referred to as 'AO' would measure one square metre, but the sizes you come across in common everyday use will be A3 (420mm x 297mm), A4 (297mm x 210mm) and A5 (210mm x 149mm). If you prepare your camera-ready copy on A4 paper, then a printer or reprographic shop will be able to reduce it if necessary. If you intend to do your own duplicating, then most reprographic systems will be able to reduce your text percentage-point by percentage-point. There are fixed reduction ratios too, of course: if I instruct my photocopier to reduce an A4 original to A5, it will switch to a 70% reduction setting of its own accord.

You might decide to print or photocopy onto sheets which you'll then fold in half at the binding stage (for example, A4 sheets folded to make A5), in which case it will be vital to think carefully about where each page will be placed in the order of things. If you were producing a mere leaflet of eight numbered pages, for example, you'd copy pages one and eight on one side of a sheet, right and left respectively, with pages two and seven on the reverse; the second sheet would have pages three and six on one side, and pages four and five on the other. This might not sound complicated, but it can become so, believe me! If you choose this option, it's probably best to make up a dummy book as a basis from which to work.

• *Style and size of type*

You can have an enormous variety of options here if you use a computer with appropriate software. If you're using a typewriter, you may have a daisy wheel or a golf ball that can be changed to give you different typefaces – or you may have no choice at all, and will have to use the type that is standard for your machine whether you are typing text, notes or headings.

Any sophisticated computer software will offer you a range of fonts, that is, styles of type. These may be called Times Roman or Dutch or something else, depending upon the manufacturer; they may be serif, sans-serif, or utterly individualistic. Type style and

Copies of documents from public archives may be used as illustrations in a family history book, providing that you obtain permission to do so and pay a fee where necessary. This certificate from the register of births originally held at Dr Williams's library is now at The National Archives (RG5/15).

size are largely a matter of personal choice, but I can't help thinking that a good classical serif face or font (that is, one where the letters have fine little lines finishing off the main strokes) would seem to be most appropriate for your journey into history.

Once you've chosen your style, you can choose the size – 'point size' in the jargon. For everyday use I go for ten or twelve-point type, but if you intend to reduce at the copying or printing stage, you'll need to experiment. Twelve-point type on an A4 sheet reduced to A5 is rather too small to be read comfortably, so start off with a larger point size. If in doubt make your type size larger; this will mean that your book will contain more pages, but nothing could be worse than the thought of your readers struggling to read the text that you've slaved over so carefully for so long.

Of course your headings can be in larger, bold type; your footnotes or notes might be in smaller type; you can use italic or bold or underlining at will. Don't overdo it, though – this is a family history, not a type-founder's specimen book! I wouldn't contemplate using a gothic or 'black letter' font (as used, for example, for the masthead of the *Daily Telegraph* newspaper) for headings; you may feel that this will give your book an olde-worlde feel, but it always looks rather precious, and some of the more extreme letter forms can be almost impossible to read!

Your computer software will almost certainly offer you options such as 'proportional spacing' and 'justified right margin'. Proportional spacing will give your text a more pleasing appearance by allowing for different widths of characters. The letter 'w', for instance, is wider than the letter 'i', but would normally be allocated the same amount of spacing. With proportional spacing, the 'w' is given more space than the 'i', creating a more even and professional appearance. As to 'justified right margin', if a margin is said to be justified, it means that your eye sees a straight line as it follows that margin down the page. The left-hand margin of any block of text will be justified (unless you have deliberately indented it) whether it's produced on a typewriter or a word processor. What a word processor (or an electronic typewriter) can do for you that a manual typewriter can't, however, is to justify the right hand margin. Perhaps it is this feature that most enables computer-set type to resemble the real old-fashioned typesetting of the past. In the days of lead type, spacers had to be inserted to make the right-hand margin of a book or newspaper appear to be in a straight line as you looked down the page. Now all this can be done electronically. What magic!

• *A running title*

You may choose to use a 'running title', which involves placing the title of the book and/or that of the relevant chapter, at the top of each page. If you do choose to use running titles in this way, you should omit them when it comes to the page which begins a chapter, or one which consists entirely or largely of illustrations. And while we're about it: do be sure to begin each chapter on a new page.

A wiredrawer at work, from The book of English trades and library of the useful arts *by Sir Richard Phillips (11th edition, 1823). Try to find an illustration which brings alive a trade practised by an ancestor.*

◆ *Some guidelines: text*

Whether you'll be preparing your text pages using a typewriter or a printer linked to your computer, there are some basic guidelines you should follow:

- *Use one side of the paper only*

This gives you maximum flexibility, and you'll avoid the risk that text which appears on the reverse side of a sheet may show through at the photocopying or printing stage.

- *Use generous margins around the edge of each master*

The term 'generous' is deliberately vague here, since you'd be wise to be guided by your own judgement, having looked at some examples of books which seem pleasing to you. A two-centimetre margin would be appropriate in most cases, though you should consider leaving a broader inner margin (for the 'gutter' of the book, as it is called) to allow for binding. Set your typewriter or word processor top, bottom and side margins accordingly. If in doubt, leave more space rather than less. Nothing is worse than a page that seems to be too full of text.

- *Leave generous spacing between the lines of text*

Give the text plenty of vertical space in which to breathe, and use an extra line-space between paragraphs if you like. If you intend to reduce your camera-ready master at the photocopying or printing stage, experiment to see what the final result will look like.

- *Avoid 'widows' and 'orphans'*

What on earth are they? A widow occurs when the last line of a paragraph appears at the top of the next page (lonely, bereaved and unloved, as it were), and an orphan is the reverse – when only the first line of a paragraph appears at the foot of one page, the remainder then continuing on the next page. Paragraphs are important building blocks in your text, and deserve better than to have their loose ends left lying around.

You may be preparing your text pages using a typewriter. If so, do aim for a good strong black print. A carbon ribbon is ideal, though more expensive in that it can be used once only.

If you're using a dot-matrix printer attached to your computer, again make sure that you have a ribbon which will give you a good clear black impression. If your inkjet or laser printer is in good working order, there should be no problems; just make sure you aren't getting stray blobs of ink or toner on the copies.

◆ *Some guidelines: illustrations*

If you're fortunate enough to have the wherewithal and the know-how to be able to scan images into the word processing or desk-top publishing programme on your computer, you won't need any hints about the creation of master copies using paste and paper.

For those not so fortunate, let's think our way through the process of creating quality master copies of pages which consist entirely or largely of illustrations. You'll need good clear masters with plenty of contrast throughout; no copying process will improve upon a poor original.

• *Prepare your master copy carefully*

Some of your illustrations may be straightforward enough (a portrait with a caption, for example) while for others you may be producing a collage of various elements, illustration and text, stuck on to a single sheet. Do bear this in mind: the important thing is that the final copies you make should be clear and clean, even if the master copy from which they are taken may look rather untidy. If you are pasting an illustration onto a blank page (do use starch paste, Cow Gum or some other adhesive which doesn't stick too firmly, too fast, and apply it thinly), it may have straight edges, in which case you may need to use correction fluid (Tippex, Snopake or whatever) or a correction strip delivered by a 'mouse' or some other dispenser to cover the edges of the illustration as they meet the background sheet. If you don't do this, you'll get unwanted lines caused by shadows. So I hope you can see what I mean by saying that an untidy-looking master may nevertheless produce good quality final copies?

Older printed books can be a useful source of copyright-free illustrations for your family history. This view of St Pancras 'New' Church in London appeared in the Encylopaedia Londinensis *in 1821, though the building was not consecrated until 7 May 1822.*

- *Use generous margins*

Margins of two centimetres or so will be ideal for your illustration pages, as for your text pages. Also allow breathing space within the page, if appropriate, especially if you're going to reduce the original in size. A crowded illustration page can look as disconcerting as a crowded text page.

You may choose to place some illustrations in a frame, leaving others to float free, as it were.

- *Create captions*

You may create a caption which will appear next to an illustration using a typewriter or computer printer, but equally you may decide to use some form of instant transferable lettering such as Letraset. This comes in an impressive array of sizes and styles, and has revolutionised graphic art in the last four decades or so. If you use such lettering, do make sure that the letters are level and evenly spaced, and do be sure to use the backing sheet to buff them after they're in position. If you don't, the whole letters or parts of letters may lift off and leave unsightly gaps. If you've made a mistake, try removing the offending letter or letters with clear sticky tape.

- *Borrow a trick from the graphic artists*

If you need to establish a horizontal or vertical level for an illustration or for text accompanying an illustration, draw a line using a light blue pencil. A faint blue line will not be reproduced at the photocopying or printing stage, so can safely be left in place on your master. Here again, you needn't worry if a master looks messy, providing the final copies are clean.

- *Use copyright-free illustrations if you need to*

Books containing such illustrations are easy to come by. Simply photocopy the picture you want, reducing it or enlarging it if necessary, and stick it on your master where you need it to be. You could use such an illustration on a text page (next to a chapter heading, for example), but don't overdo it, or the whole thing will look tacky. There is usually a very wide range of illustrations in such copyright-free books: Queen Victoria, shown head and shoulders; a crowded charabanc; a conjuror; the Houses of Parliament – and geometrical or floral designs and borders.

- *Consider using colour illustrations*

Colour photocopying (and colour scanning on a computer) is now well-established – it may still not be a cheap option for you, but it could add real quality to your book. The bad news is that photographs, colour or black and white, will not photocopy well on a black and white machine unless they are particularly strong on contrast. As an experiment, try photocopying a photograph and then a picture from a newspaper. The copy of the photograph may well look murky and thoroughly uninspiring, while the newspaper picture could give you a clear, sharp copy. Why is this? It's because the newspaper photograph has been 'screened', that is, reduced to a series of dots of varying density. If you take your book to a printer, he will screen your photographs before printing – it's one of the things you're paying him for. If you do intend to produce your book using a photocopying process, it might be worth taking your photographs to a local printer and asking what he'd charge for providing you with a screened half-tone copy of each. If the price is reasonable, you can then use the screened copies for photocopying purposes.

PUBLISHING YOUR FAMILY HISTORY

The day will dawn when you have finally completed your book in all its aspects. The family history itself is now as good as you can make it, you've added a number of extra elements comprising both text and illustrations, and you have a good quality master copy to work from. You've reached that critical stage that lies 'between product and production' (to borrow a phrase used by Ian Templeton in his book *Biographics: publish family history; inexpensive ways to do it yourself* (1982), p.68).

'Production' here simply means having copies made from the master you have created. How optimistic will you be – would fifty such copies suit your needs, or would you hope to be able to dispose of five hundred or so?

A cursory glance at a handful of 'published' family histories will give you some idea as to the range of these that exists. At one extreme will be a modest A4 publication consisting of a few sheets of paper held together with a couple of staples. At the other may be a product which has clearly cost someone (the author or his sponsor) a tidy fortune, no expense spared.

PRINTING

Here are some of the printing options which should be available to you:

◆ *Use a commercial printer*

Using a commercial printer is one option open to you. He can use your camera-ready masters (or your computer disks) to produce a professional-looking final product, grand or plain according to what you can afford.

There is no shortage of jobbing printers in today's world, many of them specifically geared up to produce short runs of books like yours. Do shop around, then, but bear in mind the advantages of dealing with someone who is located close to your home and with whom you can develop a good working relationship. Ask for a quotation for providing as many copies of your book as you will need at the outset, and enquire about the cost of any extra run-ons which you might decide you need at a later date. Don't necessarily opt for the cheapest quotation – have a look at samples of a printer's work to give you some idea as to the quality of the work he is able to produce.

It's true that a printer will only have to stand the cost of making a litho plate from your originals once, and that there is a unit-cost saving the more copies you have run off. Don't let this persuade you to have thousands of copies just for the sake of it, however!

If you decide that you can't afford to pay a short-run printer for his services, then other alternatives will need to be found.

◆ *Inkjet or laser printing*

You could run off copies of your book direct from an inkjet or laser printer, but be aware that printing from ink jets can be susceptible to damage from damp, and that laser printer toner seems very susceptible to acid in papers.

◆ *Photocopying*

Photocopying is another popular method of producing multiple copies of your book; it will cost good money, certainly, but will usually be cheaper than using a commercial printer, and you'll be working on a 'Print on demand' basis, thus avoiding the need to store huge stocks of unsold books.

You might choose to slave over a hot photocopier yourself, or else use your local reprographic shop. In either case, give some thought to the kind of paper you will use. By all means go for quality, but don't choose a really heavyweight paper that the photocopier won't like: 80gsm (grammes per square metre) or 100gsm are about the right weights to use for the bulk of your book. Pay extra for acid-free paper if you're really concerned about the durability of the final product, but avoid using glossy paper, which is highly reflective and can be difficult to read in certain light conditions.

If you will be carrying out the photocopying yourself, decide upon the reduction ratio, if any, you'll be working to. Experiment with this first just to be sure, and be aware that many photocopiers automatically revert to a standard setting if nothing seems to be happening for a while.

Once you have a huge pile of photocopied sheets, you'll then need to collate these into a number of completed books with the correct pagination. Either try and find a mechanical collator (some photocopiers will collate as they print), or enlist the help of the family – get them walking round a large table, picking up sheets as they go. You really ought to check each book at the end to be sure that pages are neither missing nor repeated.

BINDING

From the cheapest to the most expensive, your binding options will be:

◆ Staples

Using staples is a basic but effective binding method which you might consider if your book is of a modest size. I've just bought a heavy-duty stapler which will handle sixty or so sheets at a time – it's been a great boon, and was not at all expensive.

If your book consists of sheets folded down the centre, you should try to beg or borrow a long-arm stapler, and staple down the centre of the folded sheet – this is known as saddle stitching.

Some staples do rust in time, alas, and can leave a brown stain and break the paper which surrounds them. This can be repaired if necessary, but if you use staples then your book may not have the long healthy life you might have wished for.

As to covers, you could use single sheets of thin card front and back, with appropriate text and some illustration printed or photocopied on them. There are some pleasant linen-effect and laminated cards on the market, but try not to use anything too heavy for the job. It can be very effective to use a wrap-around card cover, glued to the spine.

By the way, just to make life difficult for us all, you'll find that in the printing trade a stapled book is often said to be 'stitched'.

◆ *Loose-leaf ring binder*

This is a possibility, though a rather tame one, you might think. It's cheap, and pages can be added or removed at will. The normal choice would be a two-ring binder; punch holes in the pages of your book, open the rings, insert the pages, and close the rings. Stick a sheet featuring the title and an illustration on the front cover if you like, and also a spine title.

◆ *Slide bar binder*

Another possibility if your book is not a large one is to use a slide-bar binder; this is the term I use for one of those round or triangular-shaped strips of plastic which is folded over in such a way that you can slide it up the spine to hold the book firm. You can staple the pages before you use the slide bar, or not if you prefer.

◆ *Spiral binding*

You can create a fairly solid wire spiral binding for your book, but the more usual alternative is to use a lightweight coloured plastic spiral 'comb'. A simple machine (your local college or school may let you use one) punches a series of slots on the edge of the book to be bound, and then fits the plastic comb into the slots. A spiral binding is serviceable but not very exciting, in my view, though it can accommodate a surprisingly large number of pages if necessary.

A quick glance through an office supplies catalogue may give you other ideas: 'channel' binding; 'post' binding, or the

'Professional Velobinder' which 'produces secure professionally-bound documents of up to 250 without heat or electricity. The pages are locked together with the unique patented binding strips'. It's not only family history authors who are looking for an inexpensive but durable and attractive form of binding, so do look around the world of office supplies and see what you can find.

◆ Thermal binding

Your local office supplies store will probably be able to sell you a thermal binding machine which uses heat to create a durable spine. A typical advertisement for such a machine would tell you that it 'binds up to 500 pages in seconds' and comes complete with a cooling rack. What a relief! Thermal binders are designed primarily for office use, but might suit your needs very well.

◆ Perfect binding

You might say that so-called 'perfect binding' can be anything other than 'perfect' in the wrong hands. It involves taking loose sheets and fixing them at the spine edge with a strong and flexible adhesive, after which a cover is wrapped around the entire book. This is a job that you'll need a local printer or bookbinder to do for you, but try to make sure that he uses paper which is light enough not to put strain on the spine every time the book is opened and do leave a particularly generous gutter margin on all your pages.

◆ Case binding

Although a perfect-bound book can be given a set of hard covers, true 'case binding' is in a class of its own, the Rolls-Royce model which will not come cheap. You might decide to have a few case-bound copies of your book produced – one for yourself and one for immediate family members – leaving the rest to be bound in a cheaper fashion.

If a book is case bound, it will be sewn with thread and firmly fixed within hard covers. A binder can produce a case-bound book from a stack of individual sheets of paper which you hand him, and this is something he probably does for university student theses at certain times of the year. He will sew these together, up and over, attach endpapers at the top and bottom, glue the spine, surround it with a strong cloth called mull, and then glue the book itself into the made-to-measure case which he's made of thick board and cloth. The book's title can be gold blocked onto the front cover and the spine as required.

That leaves the best-quality and most expensive binding of all, namely, the use of sewn sections – the style of binding used for centuries, long before the invention of alternative methods. A section will start off life as a large sheet of paper on which various pages of the book have been printed in a specific order, some the right way up, some upside-down. This is known as 'imposition'. The sheet is then folded – once to make a folio, twice for quarto, three times for octavo, and so on through duodecimo and the rest, depending upon the number of folds made. Each set of folded pages constitutes a section or 'signature'; all the sections will then need to be trimmed and sewn together to make the final book. The result should be a strong, durable product, easy to open, with a convex spine and a concave 'foredge', as it is called. If you take your loose camera-ready master sheets to a printer, he could use these to produce the large sheets necessary for sewn sections to be made.

Cover your case-bound book with a dustjacket, and you will have a quality product of which you can be proud and which should last for years to come. With luck it will look nice, feel nice and even smell nice. It'll leave a gaping hole in your bank balance, but you might feel that it's been worth it.

There is a fairly modern alternative to using a dustjacket as such. If you look at a number of books published in recent years, such as the Phillimore series, *Hatchments in Britain*, you'll see that instead of having plain cloth-covered boards, in effect they have a dustjacket glued to the boards and the spine, incorporated into the book and not separate from it. Laminated paper is frequently used for this purpose. This can look very handsome, and you should see whether a local printer or binder can offer you such an alternative. This is known in the trade as a 'cover for case' or 'self-covered' style.

MARKETING, ADVERTISING, DISTRIBUTION AND SELLING

You now have multiple copies of your book, printed and bound. They might be cluttering up your house or your garage, so the next imperative is to get rid of them and to get some cash in return. Let's move on to the next stage, as you become less of an author and publisher, more of a salesman.

◆ *The selling price*

Whether you've launched your book by way of a subscription list or not, you'll have copies to sell. You'll need to establish a selling price – indeed, you'll already have had to do so before printing the price on your book.

It's unlikely that you'll make a profit, but presumably you'll also want to minimise your losses. Breaking even may be your wildest ambition. Do remind yourself at this stage that your book has been your very own creative venture, and that as such has probably given pleasure not just to you but to other members of the family, too. In that sense you've already had your reward; now you'll be keen that as many people as possible should read what you've written, especially if they might be distant cousins, previously unheard-of, who might contact you with priceless new information as a result of reading what you've written.

Whilst bearing all this in mind, you might nevertheless like to draw up a mini-business plan, seeking to estimate what your unit costs per finished book have been – excluding any payment to you for your own time and trouble! Whatever such a plan might reveal, do try and keep the selling price as low as possible. It's better to sell all the books you've had printed by offering them at a very reasonable price than to be left with a pile of unsold copies which were too expensive for anyone to buy, and are now gathering dust. Don't forget that every book sold is potentially another book sold, in that each acts as its own advertisement. Distant cousin Amy visits distant cousin Betty, sees your book on the coffee table, and immediately writes to you for a couple of copies. To some extent, the more you sell, the more you're likely to sell.

◆ Who to sell to

Try as I might, I really can't avoid using the dreaded word, 'market'. There should be a market out there for your book – or rather, a series of markets. As they might say on a sales course, define your markets, inform them of your product, then sell to them. It makes sense. What markets will you have? Immediate family, wider family, friends, neighbours, libraries, interested genealogists or local historians, people living in a locality you've featured strongly, and so on.

◆ A publication date

If you really want to be as professional as possible, you should decide upon a precise publication date. Ideally, no matter how impatient you may feel, you should only release copies of your book on that day and not before. It wouldn't be unduly cynical of me to suggest that you might like to consider a date in September or October, in good time for Christmas. Your book could be used as a very welcome stocking-filler by those who have bought after-shave for their nearest and dearest more often than they would have liked.

◆ Advertising

How do you inform your potential customers of the existence of your book? By word of mouth, by letter or fax or e-mail, by means of the Internet, and/or by producing an advertising sheet known as a 'flier'. You could get copies of the front portion of your dustjacket run off as single sheets for this purpose, with advertising material printed on the back. You should try to leave a few fliers lying around wherever you go (without being a litter lout), and you could even pay to have some sent out as inserts in relevant family history journals or magazines.

You should also compose an informative and persuasive press release for appropriate newspapers or journals. Here you must give full details of the book, specifying a price (inclusive and exclusive of postage and packing, both inland and overseas) and a publication date. Give your name, address, telephone and fax or e-mail number. Give the press release a title, and try to come up with a selling angle. You can see it now, can't you: the editor of a local newspaper reads your press release, sees that a family history will include text and pictures about his or her town, contacts you for a chat, asks if it's all right to copy one of your photographs, and then runs a feature which gives you a great deal of publicity which will cost you nothing. Even the editor of the newspaper covering the area where you now live – miles away from your ancestral roots – may compose an article under the headline: 'Local woman traces her roots'.

An ounce of free publicity is worth a pound of paid advertising. Generally assume, nevertheless, that journalists are busy people: let your press release do most of the work for them, and don't be surprised if it appears in the newspaper exactly as you've written it. Why not send a press release to your local radio or television station, followed up by a telephone call a few days later?

I cannot overemphasise the importance of the judicious use of free copies. Give one book as a present to each of your nearest relatives and to those who have made a sterling contribution to the finished work. I'd go so far as to say that any copy of your book given away free will pay financial dividends in the long run. The person who receives it will feel grateful to you, others may see his or her copy and want one of their own – and everyone will generally feel warm and cosy inside. Goodwill will abound.

Not only that, but I do hope you'll wish to present a free copy of your book to an appropriate local library or record office. If you send a complimentary copy to the Society of Genealogists (14 Charterhouse Buildings, Goswell Road, London EC1M 7BA) for their library, you should also enquire whether they would consider reviewing it, or at least giving it a mention, in their *Genealogists' Magazine*. Do send a review copy to other family history and local history journals or magazines, and to the Institute of Heraldic and Genealogical Studies (Northgate, Canterbury, Kent CT1 1BA), which publishes its own journal, *Family History*.

Reviewers are usually very kind and tolerant to authors of family histories; they will have some inkling of the work involved, they'll know how much the book means to you, and although they may have a few reservations, they'll normally praise you for having taken such trouble.

Make the reviewer's life a little easier: do produce a single sheet of paper which gives full details of your book, its price (including postage and packing, home and overseas), the source of supply and a brief synopsis of the contents, and tuck this into the review copy you send. Use one of your press releases for this purpose if you like. The review itself should generate sales for you, so please don't ask for your review copy to be sent back to you!

If you are unlucky enough to get an unfavourable review, your best bet is to keep a low profile. By all means write to the journal concerned to correct an error of fact in the review, but don't get into a slanging match. Let sleeping dogs lie.

◆ Selling and distribution

So you've defined your markets, you've informed them of your book; now you've got to sell copies.

Why not throw a party to launch your masterpiece on the day of its publication? Organise one at home and invite all your friends and relations, or get some free food laid on in the village pub which is mentioned in your story, and drum up some local interest. Avoid certain times of the year like Cup Final or Election Day. Produce some posters and handouts, generally sound off a fanfare; this may be the first time your ancestral village has been featured so prominently in words and pictures in a book. Will the local publican sell some copies for you on commission, or will the vicar take a few on sale or return, pleased to receive a modest contribution to church funds? How about the local post office? Will the local building society manager give you a free window display? Can the town library help you with some publicity?

Let's assume, however, that most of the copies of your book will be distributed by post; families are now so widespread that many of your customers will live nowhere near you. Every book sold in this way will be a direct sale, and the full price will come your way. Don't be embarrassed about charging for packaging as well as postage.

112

As soon as anyone else sells for you – be it the publican, the vicar, the postmaster, a shop, a family history society, a family history magazine or whatever, you'll have to share the proceeds. A commercial retailer would normally expect to keep at least a third of the cover price, though if the books are on sale or return you should try offering less. You may feel that it is only worth using a retail outlet if doing so will enable you reach the parts you cannot reach yourself. The vicar or the Family History Society may expect less of a cut, and here you must negotiate, but if you need to use a distributor of some sort, that will cost you another 20% or so. Yes, I know, it's all very unfair ...

Normally you'd expect to sell quite a few books in the first few weeks or months, when it's all new and exciting, and when people with their ear to the ground hear the good news that your long-anticipated masterwork is finally in print. Thereafter things will probably slow down to a trickle, perking up when a review appears, or when a copy bought by someone in Australia suddenly generates some interest Down Under. Eventually you may sell out. If you do, a week later some dear sweet cousin you didn't know you had will be on the phone, desperate to buy a copy. If only you hadn't done the hard sell on people who weren't really interested, or paid the retailer his cut, you'd be better off financially and your new found cousin would be happy. Too late! It's a good policy, then, if you don't intend to go for a further print run, to keep a reserve of a dozen copies or so, only to be sold or given away in very special circumstances.

Now let me share with you a spot of good financial news ...

◆ *Value Added Tax*

At the present time (but watch this space ...) books are zero-rated for VAT in the United Kingdom. This isn't the same thing as saying that they are not subject to VAT: they are subject to it, but the current rate is zero per cent. This means that you won't have to go through the paraphernalia of charging VAT and then reclaiming it if you're eligible to do so. Not only that, but if you're paying a printer to deliver complete books to you (and he may have sub-contracted parts of the production such as typesetting and binding to someone else),

113

then his invoice should be free of VAT. A gentle reminder before he starts work might not come amiss. Why pay 17.5% extra if you don't need to?

◆ *Public Lending Right*

If your book is lodged with one or a number of libraries and is borrowed by a significant number of people, you deserve to make at least a small financial gain. After all, someone who might otherwise have bought a copy of your book may get to read it for nothing by using a public library. The rewards under the Public Lending Right arrangements won't make you rich, however. Payment is currently made at the rate of just over four pence per loan, the calculations being based on returns from a sample of lending libraries. To register and to have at least some chance of getting a few lots of four-pences, write to: Public Lending Right Office, Richard House, Sorbonne Close, Stockton-on-Tees TS17 6DA, or go to the PLR web-site at *www.plr.uk.com*

DIGITAL PUBLISHING

Writing a full-length family history and publishing it in some kind of printed or duplicated form can be a long job, and will have cost implications. Most family historians would probably take the view that one of the main purposes of any such publication would be to disseminate some of the information they have accumulated over a length of time, and that this imperative takes precedence, in the final analysis, over the sheer quality of any published book.

More modest and less expensive options are available to you, of course. I've already suggested that you might like to think in terms of short free-standing 'cameos', which may or may not be combined into a book eventually, and in any case you might feel that it was enough to produce a large or small collection of family facts, pedigrees and short biographies, a kind of resource book for researchers, rather than a narrative as such. If you do decide upon this option and if it's well indexed, it could certainly be a boon to others. You could always combine the narrative and resource book elements, the latter by way of substantial appendices, if you wish.

The very word 'publishing' seems to suggest the print medium alone, but we have steadily grown used to the idea that material can be 'published' in digital form – on a CD-ROM or on the internet. You may have noticed recently that some authors have chosen to make their latest novel available on the internet, much to the chagrin of their publishers!

The internet is certainly an option worth considering, then, and for an excellent straightforward account of how to publish on-line, with an explanation of the importance of GEDCOM (Genealogical Data Communication), HTML (Hypertext Markup Language) and the rest, you should look at chapter twelve of Peter Christian's excellent book, *The Genealogist's Internet* (2002) (an associated web-site is at *www.spub.co.uk/ protgi/*). Other books which are likely to be of interest include *Web Publishing for Genealogy* (2nd edition, 1999), also by Peter Christian, and *Publishing Your Family History on the Internet* by Richard S. Wilson (1999). Various web-sites will also be of value, including Cyndi's 'Genealogy Home Page Construction Kit' at *www.cyndislist.com/construc.htm*

The basic process of publishing a family history on the internet can be defined readily enough. Start off by defining your goals. You may simply wish to make your family tree available on a pedigree database (for a list of these, see *www.cyndislist.com/ database.htm*), and/or you might aim for a full-length family history, complete with illustrations and pedigrees, in which case you'll need to learn the basics of web creation; plan and build your site by creating pages and linking them; find a host (internet service provider) for it; set up some webspace; transfer your pages to the webspace; and then submit your web-site to as many search engines as you think appropriate so that interested family historians can find you. Does that sound simple enough? Well, you'll have plenty of new skills to learn as you go along, but you should have a lot of fun. Ideally, the site which you create should be easy to find, quick to load and simple to understand and navigate.

Once you've gone to the trouble of producing your family history in digital form, it would make sense to transfer the information onto writable CDs and give copies to relatives and to various archive repositories and libraries.

The internet, like every other publishing medium, has its advantages and disadvantages.

◆ *Advantages*

• It should be inexpensive compared to some alternative methods of publishing.

• You can feature as little or as much material as you like, and present it in a variety of different ways. Over time you can make additions and amendments to your heart's content, or change the format. In other words, you should have plenty of flexibility.

• You should reach a large number of interested family historians, especially if you get it featured on a number of search engines or can persuade other sites to provide a link to yours. Your web-site, which will be open 24 hours a day and can be advertised on all your outgoing e-mails if you wish, can be thought of as a kind of 'fishing expedition' which hopes to catch distant relatives and others who may be able to add to your own knowledge.

◆ *Disadvantages*

• Until you acquire some advanced skills, it won't be easy to make your site as attractive in appearance as a well-produced book.

• You will have little control over the material you have provided for free public access. You'd need to make special arrangements if you wanted to charge people to visit your site, and it's hard to prevent others 'stealing' as much of your work as they want to, with or without acknowledgement, even though they could well be infringing your copyright in the process.

• You could find yourself in difficulty over matters of data protection and privacy – especially if you're foolhardy enough to make substantial reference without their permission to people who are still alive. If you're not careful, there's always the chance that you may spark off, or resurrect, family feuds.

• If you grow dissatisfied with the internet service provider you're using, it may not be easy to make a change.

If you really wanted to be radical, of course, you could eschew the printed or digital alternatives completely, and feature your family history on video or as an audio-visual presentation. But maybe you wouldn't have read thus far in this book if that were your intention ... ?

Even your parents and grandparents are part of your family history! Here, the author's parents, Sidney and Beth Titford, celebrate their diamond wedding anniversary in 1990.

CONCLUSION

Can there be an appropriate conclusion to a book which exhorts you to write a family history and to publish it if you possibly can? Certainly by now I hope you will have cast aside my mocking suggestion at the start of this book that you might find the whole thing all too much for you.

I've been gratified to find that lectures I've given at various Family History Society meetings over the years, and also at a conference held in New Zealand under the title of 'Imprint 2002: Putting your family history in print', organised by Viv Parker and Keith Vautier, have persuaded at least a handful of people to lay aside all procrastination and to start writing a book they'd long intended to tackle one day. My earnest hope is that some of the readers of this book may tread the same path.

I do think it's important to make your family history findings widely available, and I do feel that you'd derive an enormous amount of satisfaction from doing it. Who knows, I may even have the pleasure of writing a review of your completed book one day? I do hope so.

ACKNOWLEDGEMENTS

The author is grateful to the following for permission to reproduce illustrations: London Metropolitan Archives (p. 14); the late Rear Admiral D. G. Titford (pp. 72 and 85); Lord Pembroke and the Trustees of the Wilton Estate, from a document now held in Wiltshire Record Officer (p. 72); the Secretary, Frome Society for Local Study (p. 75); Joan Coales Esq, (p. 88); the National Archives (p. 95); Dominic Winter Book Auctions, Swindon (p. 34).

All other illustrations are from originals held by the author.

Some, from the list of 'pros and cons' of internet publishing mentioned in this book, were taken from a presentation made at the *Imprint 2002* conference in Auckland, New Zealand, by Peter Sim of Whangerei.

INDEX

NOTES

NOTES

NOTES

NOTES